Irresistible Shakespeare

by Carol Rawlings Miller

SCHOLASTIC
PROFESSIONAL BOOKS

NEW YORK • TORONTO • LONDON • AUCKLAND • SYDNEY
MEXICO CITY • NEW DELHI • HONG KONG

Dedication

This book is for my parents, Charles and Joan Rawlings, whose years together began as Falstaff and Mistress Ford while acting in *The Merry Wives of Windsor*.

Acknowledgments

I would like to express my gratitude to the National Endowment for the Humanities and Miriam Gilbert of the University of Iowa for a spectacular summer of study at the Shakespeare Institute in Stratford-upon-Avon, England. I would also like to acknowledge other institutions where I have studied Shakespeare: LAMDA, HB Studios, and the Shakespeare Birthplace Trust. And I would like to thank Saint Ann's School for supporting my study of Shakespeare, most especially Stanley Bosworth, Linda Kaufman, and Gail Brousal.

I would also like to thank the following teachers, colleagues and friends with whom I have learned to love Shakespeare, most especially Lois Refkin, but also Sheila Allen, Jane Avrich, Bruce Baskind, Cicely Berry, Kevin Cahill, Ruth Chapman, Jim Cohan and Jane Saks Cohan, Michael Donoghue, Diane Gnagnarelli, Candace Howard Anger, William Hogeland, Shawn Nacol, Edward Rawlings, Ann Rawlings, Nancy Reardon, Robert Smallwood, Suzie Starke, and Susannah Wolk. To Jeanne and Milton Miller and to Pamela Clarke Keogh, thank you for all the encouragement.

I am grateful to Virginia Dooley and Ellen Ungaro
for their editorial expertise and also to Wendy Murray.

Finally, to my husband Jim Miller, thank you
for enjoying Shakespeare with me.

Excerpt from A WRINKLE IN TIME by Madeleine L'Engle, © 1962 by Madeleine L'Engle. Published by Bantam Doubleday Dell Publishing Group, Inc.

Cover design: Josué Castilleja
Cover illustration: David Wenzel
Interior design: Solutions by Design, Inc.

ISBN 0-439-09844-0

Table of Contents

Preface

Why This Book?

Teaching Shakespeare can be such a great pleasure; exploration of his plays can set off classroom magic. His poetry, wit, and matchless insight into the human experience can bring students and teachers together in charged literary discussions that can be in turns fascinating, moving, and thrillingly hilarious.

Teaching Shakespeare, however, can unnerve even a seasoned and confident English teacher. The most obvious sticking point is the language—the vocabulary can seem daunting, the sentence structures archaic, and the poetry difficult.

But there is another, less obvious, challenge to teaching Shakespeare. Plays are meant to be performed. Teaching drama away from its native element—the stage—can fall flat without proper attention to the special nature of dramatic writing. In Shakespeare's day, the idea of reading a play was, for a variety of reasons, basically an alien concept. Being aware of the conventions and qualities of dramatic writing in the Elizabethan period makes approaching Shakespeare's work easier and much more fun.

The Premise

The first part of this book includes teaching materials and student reproducibles that address the difficulties common to teaching Shakespeare. There are assignments that teach students how to read the poetic language, including activities that introduce meter and iambic pentameter, and there are assignments designed to sensitize students to the key elements of dramatic writing. The activities include background information, key terms, as well as discussion questions that can be used with the entire class or in small groups.

The second part of the book presents a speech study and five playlets that can be used for a focused study of Shakespeare. Since it is not always possible to read an entire play, each playlet features a scene or scenes from one of Shakespeare's plays that form a self-contained story. Each playlet is presented with enough background material to make it possible for students to read and understand without knowing the whole play. There are short scenes from *Henry V, As You Like It,* and *The Taming of the Shrew* and longer excerpts from *A Midsummer Night's Dream* and *Romeo and Juliet.*

In many cases, lines have been cut and scenes combined to bring the playlets down to a feasible size for reproducing. Every effort has been made to keep the most wonderful lines. (Cutting lines from Shakespeare to shorten scenes is a process familiar to most contemporary directors, who edit his works for the modern audience.)

How to Use This Book

Naturally, you will use what follows in whatever way is practical and useful for you. I think of using a book like this as analogous to using a cookbook; I usually incorporate recipes into my repertoire over time. One or more of the playlets can be used as part of an introduction to Shakespeare unit. Or the materials can be used to supplement the study of a play. For example, the two *Richard III* speeches are fascinating to read with students as they finish *Macbeth,* since both plays deal with a usurpation of a rightful ruler and the consequences.

Tips for Teaching Shakespeare

Following are some general tips to help you introduce Shakespeare to your class.

⊛ Encourage students to read in their own voices. Attempts at adopting an English accent simply encourage the notion that Shakespeare has nothing to do with students' lives today. As Ben Jonson said, "He was not of an age, but for all time."

⊛ If you teach meter, and there are several pages here devoted to that subject, proceed carefully. Your class may love looking at it, but if not, do not hesitate to move on.

- Remind students to figure out what is happening onstage; action often is implied in the language because Shakespeare used few stage directions. Several exercises in the next section will help students develop that skill.

- Build in time for students to memorize some lines of Shakespeare. One of the best ways for them to learn about poetry is for them to experience the sound and feeling of it firsthand, without having to look at a book.

- Let boys read girls' parts and girls read boys' parts, otherwise, with many plays, the girls will have to bow out too often.

- Have fun. When you love something, swoon over it out loud, and when something moves you, let your students know. And if a joke is bawdy, and you can do so, enjoy it with them. Your class will love Shakespeare (and you) all the more for being human.

A Few Thoughts on Teaching Shakespeare

In the middle of writing this book, life provided me with a humbling, faintly comic, and definitely useful reminder of the difficulties of teaching Shakespeare. In recent memory, my seventh-grade classes have read *Macbeth* with general pleasure. Even when they complained, it was clear that they were engaged and stimulated by Shakespeare's writing. This year I expected the same. On day three a talented—and highly vocal—student walked into class, flopped down in her seat, and proclaimed that she hated *Macbeth* and Shakespeare. I sighed. She explained that she hated how long it took to read even one page. Now, as we finish the play, she appears to be wonderfully alive to his language and ideas. Would she say she loved it? Probably not. But I hope and even sense that she will—as she becomes more confident.

Students are unaccustomed to working as hard as one does when reading Shakespeare, and some very fine young readers might resent having to experience reading as difficult again. They may think that they are regressing, just when

they have been making incredible progress by reading highly challenging verse and prose. I sometimes tell students that reading Shakespeare is the opposite of watching television, where the mind is a muscle in utter repose. When they read Shakespeare, their minds are in a state of powerful activity that will make them stronger. In the end, most students acknowledge that they are proud to be reading his work and to be included in the world of his plays, which are so deeply embedded in and important to our culture.

Great Shakespeare Resources

The Norton Shakespeare, Based on the Oxford Edition by Stephen Greenblatt (W.W. Norton, 1997). This has a useful, very readable introduction to Shakespeare's life and work, as well as introductions and notes for each play.

The Friendly Shakespeare: A Thoroughly Painless Guide to the Best of the Bard by Norrie Epstein (Penguin, 1993). In a light manner, Epstein presents wonderful anecdotal information about various productions of the plays.

The Actor and His Text by Cicely Berry, the voice director for the Royal Shakespeare Company (Virgin Publishing, 1987). This book illuminates how actors work to interpret Shakespeare's text.

Teaching Shakespeare—Yes You Can by Lorraine Hopping Egan (Scholastic Professional Books, 1998). This includes numerous ideas appropriate for work with younger students.

All Arden editions of the plays, which have extensive notes and explanatory information.

The First Folio, a facsimile edition, published by Applause Books in a soft-cover edition.

The Internet has sites too numerous to name that can be of great help, including text that you can down load and use for classroom study. Simply try www.Shakespeare.com.

Cracking Open a Play

Familiarize students with two types of openings in Shakespeare's plays.

On the Reproducible

The opening scenes from *Romeo and Juliet* and *The Taming of the Shrew*

About the Exercise

This exercise familiarizes students with two common types of openings used in plays, prologues and *in medias res*, and how each of these styles sets the stage for what follows.

Romeo and Juliet opens with a prologue in the classical mode that provides an overview of the play's "two-hours' traffic." In it we are informed that two feuding families bury their strife only after two children, one from each family, fall in love and eventually take their own lives. These two are the famous "star-crossed lovers." This type of opening provides a general overview of what we are about to see.

The form is a sonnet (14 lines of iambic pentameter with an *ababcdcdefefgg* rhyme scheme). The dignified tone and formal poetic mode are in keeping with the seriousness of a tragedy

The Taming of the Shrew opens *in medias res*. We are thrown into the middle of an argument between a lady barkeep, called the Hostess, and Sly, who is clearly drunk and disorderly. He has broken some glasses; he wants the Hostess to be quiet; he is committing a number of comical malapropisms. This scene does not provide us with any obvious clues as to the subject of the play. (In fact, this scene is from the Induction and is not part of the famous tale of Kate and Petruchio.) However, it does the important job of setting the tone and telling the audience that they are in store for a comedy.

The form is prose dialogue. There is no meter or rhyme here, which makes its rhythms more informal, suitable for comedy, and perfect for conveying realistically Sly's state of inebriation.

Key Terms

prologue: a speech at the beginning of the play that usually introduces the subject matter of the drama.

in medias res: literally "in the middle of things," *in medias res* occurs when a story or scene begins in the middle of things, before the plot has been laid out.

What to Do

First, distribute and read aloud to your students the prologue from *Romeo and Juliet*. Try to get general reactions to the speech before moving to more specific questions. Use the following Discussion Questions to spark further inquiry into the meaning and tone of the speech. Finally, summarize the meaning of the speech together and then ask a student to read it out loud. Then proceed in the same fashion with the opening from *The Taming of the Shrew*.

Discussion Questions for *Romeo and Juliet*

1 Where is the play taking place? *In Verona.*

2 The two households have an "ancient grudge." Are they friendly with each other? *They are not; an "ancient grudge" marks their friendship.*

3 The "loins" of these families produce what? *A pair of lovers.*

4 Does the play seem to be tragic or comic? *Tragic, because it includes a reference to the suicides of two young people, which is obviously serious.*

5 What do we understand that the play will be about? How much is the playwright telling us up front? *The "two-hours' traffic" will be the story of the two young lovers. The playwright is straightforward about the subject of this play and its plot.*

Discussion Questions for *The Taming of the Shrew*

1 What do you think the characters are doing as this scene opens? What is Sly's state of mind? What has he been doing at the pub? Why does he mix up his words? *He is drunk and consequently misspeaks.*

2 How were the glasses broken, do you imagine? *Possibly Sly has thrown them in a fight or at the Hostess when she asked for payment.*

3 Why does Sly say "Sessa!"? What pose do you suspect he is in as the scene ends? *Her shouting hurts his drunken ears. Sly is possibly sitting down, refusing to move.*

4 Who is "him" in the last line? *The constable.*

5 Would you say, based on this scene, that this play is likely to be comic or tragic? *The scene is funny and raucous; there aren't any hints of serious themes, which is suggestive of comedy.*

Drawing Conclusions

Ask students to reflect on the difference between the two openings. How does each make them feel? Which is livelier? Which is more serious? You might point out to students that sometimes Shakespeare leads us very carefully and clearly into a story with prologues or with long speeches. Sometimes, however, he just throws us in and gets us interested with a scene that is funny, scary, or suspenseful.

As you explore both openings with students, note that generalizing about Shakespeare can be tricky. For example, you can't say that tragedies

always open with prologues. *Hamlet* opens *in medias res*. In addition, plays can open in ways other than with a prologue or *in medias res*. They sometimes open with soliloquies, which can introduce a character and help set up the story. For example, *Richard III* opens with the famous "Now is the winter of our discontent" soliloquy (see page 30). Shakespeare used dramatic conventions in various ways to create different effects.

Teaching Tip

Consider reading speeches or bits of scenes aloud to your students before handing out reproducibles; this will expose them to the art of listening carefully for content and tone.

Related Activity

A Reading Warm-Up

Before you begin reading a play or playlet, write down short phrases from the first page of the play on slips of paper. Give each student a slip of paper and have him or her memorize the phrase on the slip of paper. Have students stand in a circle, then toss a ball or small stuffed animal to a student who will then say his line. That student should then toss the ball to another student who says his or her line and so on, going more and more quickly. Then, stop tossing and, moving in order around the circle, have each student say his line loudly while making a gesture. Then, go around a second time, and have each student whisper her line as if it were a secret. Ask students what ideas the words and phrases give them. This exercise helps students become accustomed to the opening words and phrases of the play and less fearful when they actually begin reading it.

Cracking Open a Play

Below are two passages from the opening scenes of *Romeo and Juliet* and *The Taming of the Shrew*. Read each passage, and think about how each one sets the stage for the rest of the play.

Prologue from *Romeo and Juliet*

CHORUS: Two households, both alike in dignity
In fair Verona, where we lay our scene,
From ancient grudge break to new *mutiny*,   unrest
Where civil blood makes civil hands unclean.
From forth the fatal loins of these two foes
A pair of star-crossed lovers take their life,
Whose misadventurous piteous overthrows
Doth with their death bury their parents' strife.
The fearful passage of their death-marked love
And the continuance of their parents' rage,
Which *but* their children's end, naught could remove   except for
Is the two-hours' traffic of our stage;
The which if you with patient ears attend,
What here shall miss, our toil shall strive to mend.

Opening scene from *The Taming of the Shrew*

outside a pub

SLY: I'll *feeze you*, in faith.   get you

HOSTESS: A pair of stocks°, you *rogue*.   tramp

SLY: You're a baggage. The Slys are no rogues. Look in the
Chronicles—we came in with Richard Conqueror,
therefore paucas pallabris, let the world slide.° *Sessa*!   Quiet!

HOSTESS: You will not pay for the glasses you have burst?

SLY: No, not a *denier*. Go by, Saint Jeronimy! Go to thy cold
bed and warm thee.   small coin

HOSTESS: I know my remedy, I must go and fetch the *thirdborough*.   constable

SLY: Third or fourth or fifth borough, I'll answer him
by the law. I'll not budge an inch, boy. Let him
come, and kindly.

° The stocks: a wooden device for punishing disturbers of the peace by restraining their ankles.

° Sly makes two slips of speech: "paucas pallabris" is really "pocas palabras," meaning few words, and Richard Conqueror refers to William the Conqueror, to whom the "best" English families like to claim relation.

What's Novel About a Play?
What's at Play in a Novel?

Students explore and define the difference between narrative fiction and drama.

On the Reproducible

The openings of *A Wrinkle in Time* and *Macbeth*

About the Exercise

Students are more accustomed to reading novels and stories. This exercise makes explicit the substantial change they will make when reading a play instead of a novel or a story. In a play, our sense of time, place, and character is created differently.

What to Do

Read the passages from *Macbeth* and *A Wrinkle in Time* aloud and use the following Discussion Questions to explore the two passages. Then invite students to talk about anything they notice; students often come up with great ideas. You might point out that settings, characters, and suspense are important elements of storytelling, but plays and novels often use different techniques to convey each of these elements.

In a novel the story might be told by a character, so the reader knows what the character is thinking, or the novel might have a narrator who can move inside the minds of different characters. The author can use descriptive passages to develop the setting and build suspense.

In a play, a character's personality can be inferred through the dialogue. Sometimes, a character's secret or private thoughts can be conveyed in asides or soliloquies. Stage directions and the set design are used to help set the scene.

Discussion Questions

1 What is similar about these scenes? What dramatic device do they both use to create excitement? *Both scenes begin with a storm and use the weather to create a sense of tension and excitement.*

2 Which one shows us the thoughts of a character clearly? A Wrinkle in Time *does; in it we very clearly hear Meg thinking about herself and her predicament.*

3 From reading the passages here, which scene best conveys the sense of a terrible storm? Why? Wrinkle *creates a highly vivid sense of storm, because in a novel creating a sense of setting is done with words. In a play, set designers would help fill the stage with the storm.*

4 Which scene is tempting us more with references to future events? *In* Macbeth *there is direct reference to future events; there will be a battle that involves an important character named Macbeth. In* Wrinkle *a sense of future events is less prominent, though the scene creates tension and Meg's words make us curious about her.*

Teaching Tip

Encourage students to be attentive to references to weather and location when they are reading Shakespeare. Ask them to imagine the scene and speculate on the mood that the weather and location create and how that mood relates to the action.

What's Novel About a Play?
What's at Play in a Novel?

Novels and plays are both forms of storytelling, but they do it differently. Below you will find the opening passages of a novel and a play. Read them, and think about the similarities and differences.

It was a dark and stormy night.

    In her attic bedroom Margaret Murry, wrapped in an old patchwork quilt, sat on the foot of her bed and watched the trees tossing in the frenzied lashing of the wind. Behind the trees clouds scudded frantically across the sky. Every few moments the moon ripped through them, creating wraithlike shadows that raced along the ground.

    The house shook.

    Wrapped in her quilt, Meg shook.

    She wasn't usually afraid of the weather.—It's not just the weather, she thought.—It's the weather on top of everything else. On top of me. On top of Meg Murry doing everything wrong.

    School. School was all wrong.

A Wrinkle in Time **by Madeleine L'Engle**

Thunder and lightning. Enter three witches.

FIRST WITCH:	When shall we three meet again? In thunder, lightening, or in rain?
SECOND WITCH:	When the hurly-burly's done, When the battle's lost and won.
THIRD WITCH:	That will be ere the set of sun.
FIRST WITCH:	Where the place?
SECOND WITCH:	Upon the heath.
THIRD WITCH:	There to meet Macbeth.
FIRST WITCH:	I come, Grimalkin.
SECOND WITCH:	Paddock calls.
THIRD WITCH:	Anon!
ALL:	Fair is foul, and foul is fair Hover through the fog and filthy air.

Macbeth 1.1

> **Did You Know?**
> Madeleine L'Engle refers to Shakespeare's *Hamlet*, *The Tempest*, and *Macbeth* in her classic novel, *A Wrinkle in Time*.

What's Happening?
A Close Reading Exercise

Tune students in to the clues about action taking place onstage and the characters' reactions that are embedded in the text.

On the Reproducible

Exchanges from *The Tempest, Macbeth,* and *As You Like It*

About the Exercise

Because Shakespeare used few stage directions, modern actors and directors must sometimes study the characters' lines like a puzzle to piece together the action that is happening onstage and the characters' reactions. Clues to how characters are reacting are often revealed in dialogue. If, for example, Jill says to Jack "Don't start crying," then we know that Jack is showing all the signs of tearing up.

What to Do

Explain to students that a director interprets the text of a play to help the actors create a production that makes sense. Here students will have the chance to think like a director. First, pick different students to read the scene snippets out loud. Then, have students read the passages again on their own and try to answer the questions on the reproducible. Students must work from clues in the language, just as directors do, to figure out what's happening. Finally, as a group, try to piece together what is happening in the scene.

Basic answers to the questions on the reproducible follow, but you and your students may discover more together, which is wonderful. Different interpretations of text have given rise to very different productions of Shakespeare's plays.

Answers to the Reproducible

The Tempest: Gonzalo, Antonio, and Sebastian are on a ship that is sinking. Antonio seems to be loyal, and Sebastian interested in saving his own skin. Gonzalo is on board the ship, perhaps leaning over the deck railing, though not necessarily: Get students to speculate.

Macbeth: Macbeth, assisted by Lady Macbeth, has killed the king and two guardsmen. He is dazed, apparently lost in thought and probably in shock after the murders he has committed. Lady Macbeth, however, wants to avoid thinking about the wrong they have done and appears worried that Macbeth will be paralyzed by his troubled thoughts.

Macbeth: Here a wounded, bleeding soldier arrives onstage. He has come, it would appear, from the frontline and can tell the king about the state of the revolt.

As You Like It: Ganymede faints at the sight of blood right before Celia says "Why how now Ganymede!" Ganymede regains consciousness and at the end of the scene is either getting up or is about to get up with help from Oliver at the instruction of Celia.

Teaching Tip

I approach this exercise as if it were a game, and, in fact, students often enjoy this way of looking at the text. This exercise reinforces careful reading and helps students change their expectations about how quick and easy reading Shakespeare will be. They need to learn to shift gears and begin to read more carefully.

What's Happening?

Read the following passages, and look for clues about the setting and situation, as well as the physical movements, moods, and emotional states of the characters.

MARINERS: Mercy on us—
We split, we split!—Farewell, my wife and children!
Farewell, brother! We split, we split, we split!

ANTONIO: Let's all sink with the King.

SEBASTIAN: Let's take leave of him.

[Exit]

GONZALO: Now I would give a thousand furlongs of sea for an acre of barren ground—
long heath, brown furze, anything. The wills above be done, but I would fain
die a dry death.   *(The Tempest)*

Questions: What is happening in this scene? Where are the characters? What is suggested about the characters of Antonio and Sebastian? Where do you imagine Gonzalo when he speaks those last lines?

MACBETH: Listening their fear, I could not say "amen"
When they did say, "God bless us!"

LADY MACBETH: Consider it not so deeply.

MACBETH: But wherefore could I not pronounce "Amen"?
I had most need of blessing, and "Amen"
Stuck in my throat.   *(Macbeth)*

Questions: What do you think might be happening here? Why might "Amen" stick in Macbeth's throat? What is Macbeth's state of mind in this scene? What do you make of Lady Macbeth's state of mind? Why do you think she doesn't want Macbeth to consider it "so deeply"?

DUNCAN: What bloody man is that? He can report
As seemeth by his plight, of the revolt
The newest state?   *(Macbeth)*

Questions: Who do you guess is arriving on stage and in what condition is he? Where is he coming from?

CELIA: Why how now Ganymede! Sweet Ganymede!

OLIVER: Many will *swoon* when they do look on blood.   faint

CELIA: There's more in it. Cousin Ganymede!

OLIVER: Look, he recovers.

GANYMEDE: I would I were at home.

CELIA: We'll lead you hither. I pray you, will you take him by the arm?

(As You Like It)

Questions: What is happening to Ganymede? Can you pinpoint when exactly it happens? What happens next to Ganymede? What happens at the end of the exchange?

Detective Work

Teach students to read between the lines to look for clues about character and situation.

On the Reproducible

Scenes from *Much Ado About Nothing* and *All's Well That Ends Well*

About the Exercise

Shakespeare provided no descriptions or notes on his characters. When actors and directors put on a play by Shakespeare, they must look carefully at the play to learn about who the characters are and to determine the relationships between the characters. This exercise asks students to read carefully and, without many clues, to figure out the gender and status of the speakers, their relationship, the general situation, and any action that is taking place.

What to Do

Look at the scene snippets one at a time. Select students to read the scenes and have them discuss what information they can determine, even without knowing the name of the play or the story line. Descriptions of the two scenes presented on the reproducible follow.

Answers to the Reproducible

Scene 1

In this scene from *Much Ado About Nothing* supposedly confirmed bachelorette Beatrice and bachelor Benedick have a brief exchange. Earlier in the play they had both professed disdain for the other, but, in fact, they love each other. When Beatrice appears in this scene, she is annoyed at having to talk to Benedick. But Benedick's friends have recently convinced him that Beatrice actually loves him and acts gruff to protect herself from getting hurt. He wonders if she is simply hiding her affection and, as hopeful lovers do, Benedick tries to decipher her utterances like a code. They are on par in terms of class.

Scene 2

In this scene Helena, Speaker B, is trying to hide from the Countess, Speaker A, that she is in love with her son, Bertram. Helena believes because she is not of aristocratic birth, as Bertram and the Countess are, that the confession of her true feelings will offend her noble mistress.

Teaching Tips

- Occasionally ask students to trace the antecedents of pronouns as they read. This will begin to attune them to the complexity of the language and give them a strategy for fighting against getting lost in the text.

- Encourage students to guess at what unknown words mean. Students may become unduly concerned about words they do not know. Show them how to use context clues to figure out the meaning. If they look up every word (not that many will do so), they will have to read too slowly and may become discouraged.

Detective Work

Shakespeare's texts provided no direct notes on character. Clues about character status, personality, and situation are contained in the play itself. You just have to read between the lines. Look at the scenes below, and try to figure out the gender, class, and relative status of each speaker. Then try to decipher what the situation is.

Scene 1

A: Against my will I am sent to bid you to come in to dinner.

B: Fair Beatrice, I thank you for your pains.

A: I took no more pains for those thanks than you take pains to thank me. If it had been painful I would not have come. *[Exit]*

B: Ha! Against my will I am sent to bid you come in to dinner? There's a double meaning in that.

Questions:

1. In what sort of mood does Speaker A seem to be?

2. What is the gender of Speaker A? Where is the best clue as to Speaker B's gender? What is it?

3. Why might Speaker B be looking for "double meanings"? What do you think the situation is? Why might this simple exchange of information take as long as it does?

Scene 2

A: Do you love my son?

B: Your pardon, noble mistress.

A: Love you my son?

B: Do not you love him, madam?

A: Go not about. My love hath in't a bond
Whereof the world takes note. Come, come, disclose
The state of your affection, for your passions
Have to the full *appeached*.   revealed you

B: Then I confess,
Here on my knee, before high heaven and you,
That before you, and next unto high heaven,
I love your son.
My friends were poor but honest; so's my love.

Questions:

1. Who seems to be taking the lead in the discussion? Who is older?

2. Who is of higher status?

3. Why do you think Speaker B wanted to avoid the confession of her love?

Pop-Up Language

This assignment asks students to focus on the power and purpose of imagery in Shakespeare's dramatic writing.

On the Reproducible

Passages from *Hamlet* and *A Midsummer Night's Dream*

About the Exercise

Today, when students attend a movie such as *Jurassic Park,* they can, thanks to computer graphics, see dinosaurs roaming the Earth. Shakespeare, however, wrote before the lightbulb existed. In his time, stage lights could not even be dimmed to signal the start of a play. Playwrights had to use language to draw pictures in the listener's mind. Shakespeare's language—especially when characters narrate or describe scenes—is often intensely poetic, and features highly detailed, and sometimes fantastical, imagery. The passages on the reproducible demonstrate the visual elements of Shakespeare's writing.

What to Do

The goal here is for students to become attuned to the way language can operate on the imagination. Together read and discuss what each passage makes students see, feel, and imagine.

As students read the *Midsummer* passage, make sure they understand that Robin Goodfellow (also known as Puck) is a fairy. Ask them how magical creatures and supernatural events are shown in films today. How is this passage different? Are there any disadvantages to the special effects they have seen in movies or on television? Have they ever seen unsatisfing or cheesy film effects? (Often they have quite a few to share.) Then, discuss with them what advantages language has over film. You might enrich the discussion by asking them if they have ever disliked the movie version of a beloved book. What happens when someone else interprets something they have imagined?

After students have discussed the scene from *Hamlet*, you might explain how highly dramatic scenes, such Ophelia's death, are often reported by a character because they would be difficult to stage and because they create an opportunity for a bit of highly dramatic storytelling.

If your students have completed The Poetry Tool Kit, have them also identify and discuss examples of metaphors, similes, alliteration, and personification in the passages.

Related Activities

A Monologue from a Mischief-Making Sprite

To elaborate on this assignment, have students write a monologue from a modern-day mischief-making sprite. This fairy should tell about all the secret and amazing things she can do, and all the impossible places she can get to because she is a fairy. Encourage students to be as highly detailed and fanciful as Shakespeare is.

Shakespeare-Inspired Art

Many passages in Shakespeare are unforgettably visual and have inspired artists. There are many paintings of the fairies from *A Midsummer Night's Dream*. John Everett Millais' pre-Raphaelite painting of Ophelia's drowning influenced how directors have presented the scene of Ophelia's death. You might share prints of these works with students after they have worked with these passages or invite them to illustrate their own versions.

Name _____ Date _____

Pop-Up Language

Shakespeare wrote before film and television existed. Instead he used language to spark the imaginations of the listeners and transport them beyond their present lives. Words, not computer graphics, took audiences to impossible places.

Robin Goodfellow, a mischief-making sprite, describes himself:

> I am that merry wanderer of the night.
> I jest to *Oberon*, and make him smile   fairy king
> When I a fat and bean-fed horse *beguile*,   trick, fool
> Neighing in likeness of a filly foal;
> And sometimes lurk I in a gossip's bowl
> In very likeness of a roasted crab,
> And when she drinks, against her lips I bob,
> And on her withered *dewlap* pour the ale.   fold in the neck

> ### A Midsummer's Night Dream

Queen Gertrude describes the drowning of Ophelia:

> There is a willow grows *aslant* a brook   alongside
> That shows his *hoar* leaves in the glassy stream.   whitish grey
> Therewith fantastic garlands did she make
> Of crow-flowers, nettles, daisies, and long purples,
> That liberal shepherds do give a grosser name,
> But our cold maids do dead men's fingers call them.
> There on the pendant boughs her *crownet* weeds   coronet
> Clamb'ring to hang, an envious sliver broke,
> When down the *weedy trophies* and herself   garlands
> Fell in the weeping brook. Her clothes spread wide,
> And mermaid-like a while they bore her up.

> ### Hamlet

Discussion Questions

1. What is each passage about?

2. What do you picture as you read each passage? What images does each passage create?

3. How does each one make you feel? What kind of mood do the words create in each passage?

4. Which images are most striking to you?

Teaching Meter
Six Frequently Asked Questions

The activities in the following section introduce students to meter and scansion, as well as the poetic forms iambic pentameter and trochaic tetrameter. A number of issues can crop up while trying to teach meter. Here are the answers to some frequently asked questions.

Q. Why did Shakespeare write in meter?

A. Although we can't say for certain, writing in verse was typical of the Elizabethan period and was part of the tradition of dramatic writing. The ancient classical playwrights also composed their works in meter. For dramatic purposes meter has several advantages. The sound of well-spoken metrical language is very involving. Meter creates part of the verbal texture of the play and lends to its auditory sensuousness and heightened quality. In addition, the rhythms of metered speech make it easier to memorize, and from what we know about the Elizabethan stage, actors had a great deal to learn, and often quickly.

Q. How do we know he meant to write in meter? Aren't we just overanalyzing this? Aren't you just making this up?

A. These time-honored and potentially irksome questions can actually be difficult to answer well. It is generally useful to point out that to write in verse was as normal for Elizabethan playwrights as it is for modern authors *not* to write in verse. Meter allowed the writer to play with the language in a way that helped create meaning and character. The form was very familiar to sixteenth-century audiences. Educated people during the Elizabethan age studied rhetoric and were well versed in all kinds of complexities having to do with language. Clearly though, Elizabethans did not converse in iambic pentameter any more than we chat in the cute rhythms of TV sitcoms.

Finally, and this is often the most persuasive argument, it would be a rather huge and startling coincidence if Shakespeare wrote in this iambic pattern accidentally. Students tend to associate the arts with free expression and may view meter as a conspiracy invented by teachers, contrary to expressiveness and freakishly difficult. In fact, writing in iambs is a skill that one can learn and employ with increasing ease over time.

Q. Why are there short lines in odd places?

A. Often the speech of a character ends midway through a line. The next speaker will finish that line of iambic pentameter. Characters can be said to "line share" (though it is not something *they* are doing—Shakespeare is). For example, here Tranio and Lucentio, characters from *The Taming of the Shrew*, are plotting together:

LUCENTIO:
    I have it, Tranio.

TRANIO: Master, for my hand.
    Both our inventions meet and jump in one.

Lucentio begins a line, but uses only six out of ten syllables; Tranio finishes the line (and adds an extra syllable).

Q. Why aren't all the lines in iambic pentameter the same length?

A. For a variety of reasons, some of which may not have been consciously intended, though there are many theories as to the effects of short or long lines. Some people speculate that subtle emotional shadings are created by these changes. England's Original Shakespeare Company, which tries to recreate the actual conditions in which the plays were performed, speculates that a very short line may indicate a moment where some physical action is to take place.

Q. Why does Shakespeare change the meter in a line of iambic pentameter?

A. Sometimes a poet will reverse the meter in a metrical foot. In the case of iambic pentameter, this means using a trochee instead of an iamb. When Shakespeare does this, it often occurs at the beginning of a line and is used to create emphasis. Here Ophelia speaks about Hamlet; she thinks he has gone crazy:

> Now see that noble and most sovereign reason
>
> Like sweet bells jangled out of tune and harsh;
>
> That unmatched form and feature of blown youth
>
> Blasted with ecstasy. O woe is me.

The last line begins with a reversed foot; instead of an iamb we have a stressed and then an unstressed syllable: BLASTed. Also, notice that "blasted" is the strongest word that opens a line. The Elizabethan line generally begins with a small, colorless word and ends with an interesting one. In part this happens because it is easier to begin an iambic line with a smaller unstressed syllable that leads to a stressed one. When Shakespeare begins a line with a trochee, the word is generally a stronger one.

Q. Why does Shakespeare sometimes use a rhyme at the end of a scene?

A. Shakespeare sometimes uses rhyming couplets at the end of a scene or a section of action. A rhyming couplet will often underscore an important idea or point to some future action. A couplet can emphasize an action to come by making it ring in the ears of the listeners. It may also heighten suspense. When Macbeth heads off to prepare to murder Duncan, he says:

> Hear it not, Duncan, for it is a **knell**
>
> That summons you to heaven or to **hell.**

The Music of Language
The Fundamentals of Meter

Step by step, this exercise builds toward an understanding of meter and how to scan it.

On the Reproducibles

Words, phrases, and lines for easy scansion practice

About the Exercise

Your first hurdle in building an understanding of meter is to get students to hear the stresses in a single word. The next hurdle is to have students scan phrases and then lines. In this phase of learning to scan, they need to begin to see that an iamb can, and often does, spread over more than one word. The word **rePEL** is an iamb, but the two words **it SMELLS** also make an iamb.

Depending on how strong your class is, students can work on this reproducible alone, but it is also an assignment that can be fun, and less intimidating, to do together.

What to Do

Before students begin working on the reproducible, try scanning a few words with them. Ask them to name words, and write their responses on the board or try these: **purpose, along, confuse, exist.** Then, scan the words together.

As you go over the reproducible, encourage students to read the words aloud, including the ones that are already scanned. This will help them to connect the stress marks with the sound the word makes. You may well find, however, that some will have a great deal of trouble hearing which syllable they stress; they may believe they are stressing a syllable when they are not. For example, if the word is *watermelon*, a student may think he is saying **waTERmelon**, not **WAterMElon.** You can rectify this error by saying both the correct and incorrect pronunciations in an exaggerated manner. Usually a student will hear that he is not really saying **waTERmelon.** If students are having trouble, have them consult the dictionary to clear up matters of stress. A dictionary will clarify that these are not matters of opinion, though it may provide more than one pronunciation.

Also, be aware that regional differences in pronunciation can occasionally cause controversies. (For example, Americans say **CONtroVERsies,** but the English say **conTROverSIES).**

Teaching Meter and Scansion

The most important thing about scansion is to relax when teaching it: You can easily lose the forest for the trees. Scansion can be difficult, and I have found that students can slip very easily from hating scansion to seeing Shakespeare as old-fashioned and annoyingly complex. You simply want your students to *begin* to have an understanding of meter; if more than that happens, that's great. I might spend a period or two with a class on meter, first introducing it and then playing around with scansion. I gear the amount of time I spend on meter to a class's interest level, patience, and general academic strength. If students seems highly resistant or bored, I move on and refer to it when it might be interesting. (For example, I might refer to it when there is a use of trochaic tetrameter, a shift from poetry to prose, or a significant metrical variation within a speech).

Answers to the Reproducible

pineapple	Cole Porter	Jack Sprat
prepare	yesterday	arise
shepherd	formal	Danielle

A summer's day   vacation came

the little love god   lying once asleep

this party does not tickle

I wish vacation came each day all year.

The little love god lying once asleep.

"The little love god" is Shakespeare's line.

Name _____ Date _____

The Music of Language
The Fundamentals of Meter

All English words have rhythms, because the syllables are either stressed or unstressed. When people say the vampire line *I want to suck your blood,* some of the syllables are stressed: i *WANT* to *SUCK* your *BLOOD*. If we say that same line with each syllable stressed the same way, the effect is unnatural, as if a robot were speaking: **I WANT TO SUCK YOUR BLOOD.**

The way words are pronounced has to do, in part, with this matter of stress. In the words below, the syllables in capitals are stressed; the lowercase syllables are unstressed.

> We say **PIMple** not **pimPLE**
>
> and
>
> **RUMpelSTILLskin** not **RumPELSTILLskin**
>
> and
>
> **PANcakes** not **panCAKES**

Scansion is the formal system for marking words according to stress without using capital letters. You make a — for a stressed syllable and a ∪ for an unstressed syllable. Take a look:

reveal   fabulous   approach

genius   pizza   hip hop

If you are confused by which syllables are stressed in a word, you can clarify matters by playing with different pronunciations of the word. It can help to remind yourself of how a word is most certainly not pronounced. Symphony, for example, is pronounced **SYMphony** not **symPHOny**, so you know to scan that word like this: symphony

Read over the following words and names and try to scan them.

pineapple	Cole Porter	Jack Sprat
prepare	yesterday	arise
shepherd	formal	Danielle

Write your name on the line below, and try to scan it.

_____

Irresistible Shakespeare Scholastic Professional Books

The Music of Language
The Fundamentals of Meter

Meter is the steady rhythm that is created when syllables are stressed in a systematic pattern. Poetry or verse is composed of lines written in meter.

The meter Shakespeare most often used is based on the iamb. An iamb has two syllables: The first is unstressed, and the second is stressed, like in the word *applause* (a PPLAUSE). Look at the words you scanned on the previous page. Can you find three iambs?

Another meter Shakespeare used less often is based on the trochee. A trochee also has two syllables, but it is a reversed iamb. It begins with a stressed syllable, followed by an unstressed syllable. There is one trochee in the list on the previous page. Can you find it?

This phrase has been scanned. A vertical line separates every iamb.

when hot|dogs kill

Notice in this phrase how one iamb begins with one word and ends in the next one.

a Mar|tian me|lody

Now it's your turn. Try scanning the following phrases:

a summer's day

the little love god

vacation came

lying once asleep

this party does not tickle

Now scan these ten-syllable lines:

I wish vacation came each day all year.

The little love god lying once asleep.

The last two lines are written in the most popular English meter, iambic pentameter, which has five iambs in it. Can you guess which line Shakespeare wrote?

Poetry and Prose

This activity familiarizes students with the different forms in which Shakespeare wrote.

On the Reproducibles

On the first reproducible, passages from *Romeo and Juliet*, *Macbeth*, and *Much Ado About Nothing*. On the second reproducible, an overview of iambic pentameter.

About the Exercise

Shakespeare liked to write his plays in metered speech, though not exclusively; he also wrote in prose. Students can familiarize themselves with these kinds of writing and, if you wish, practice poetic scansion with very easy examples.

Verse: Lines written in meter are also said to be written in verse or poetry. When Shakespeare does write in verse, he usually uses iambic pentameter, but he sometimes writes in shorter lines, often employing a meter called trochaic tetrameter, especially with characters using spells or employing various kinds of magical or enchanted speech. Trochaic tetrameter, which is almost always rhymed, sounds less natural, more noticeably poetic, and feels as though it has a heavy beat.

Prose: Prose is language that is not written in a formal meter. Prose tends to be akin to what we would consider "normal" speech. History books, essays, articles, stories, and novels are written in prose. In Shakespeare's work prose is used at different times. Although it is often said that lower-class characters speak in prose, this is not, in fact, a very useful generalization (though sometimes it is true). Prince Hamlet and King Lear, both of royal birth, use prose at times. Often characters will speak in verse some of the time and poetry on other occasions. Prose is also used for more informal conversations.

What to Do

Read over the three passages on the Poetry and Prose reproducible with students, and review the differences in form. As a follow-up, have students review Iambic Pentameter: What's So Great About It Anyway? to explore iambic pentameter in greater depth.

If time permits, use the examples of meter on the Poetry and Prose reproducible to practice scansion (both examples are fairly regular). Have them scan in three steps:

1 Count the number of syllables in each line, and write that number at the end of the line. You might point out that ten-syllable lines are usually written in iambic pentameter.

2 Scan the syllables to determine the kind of meter.

3 Draw a line after each metrical foot.

Properly scanned verse, with the feet marked off, looks like this:

How art|thou out|of breath|when thou|hast breath

Teaching Tip

When you teach a play, ask students to speculate on why Shakespeare switches from poetry to prose. I sometimes review the places where the changes occur after we have read a few acts. Inform students that it is often said that only lower-class characters speak in prose. Ask them, as they read a work, to test that theory. See if they can come up with a better generalization. This makes them more active readers and encourages critical thinking.

Poetry and Prose

Shakespeare liked to write in meter, mostly in iambic pentameter, though not exclusively. He also wrote in trochaic tetrameter and in prose, the style you use most often in school. Read over the following three examples, and explore their differences. These examples illustrate the different forms he used in his plays.

Iambic pentameter has ten syllables in each line. In every line there are five feet, or sections, of iambs. It goes: daDum daDum daDum daDum daDum. An iamb is two syllables, the first unstressed, the second stressed. This is the most common meter used in his plays.

Here Juliet scolds her nurse, who has postponed news of Juliet's boyfriend because she is out of breath. Juliet impatiently replies to her nurse's complaint about breathlessness:

> How art thou out of breath, when thou hast breath
>
> To say to me that thou art out of breath?

Trochaic tetrameter is made of four feet of trochees in each line. A trochee is two syllables, the first is stressed, the second unstressed. It goes: Dumdi Dumdi Dumdi Dumdi. The following words are trochees: mixing, purple, milkshakes, nightly ("Mixing purple milkshakes nightly" is trochaic tetrameter). Often these lines are rhymed in couplets at the end. Shakespeare used this meter occasionally, usually for magical or enchanted speech.

Here, three witches in *Macbeth* chant over their potent brew:

> Double, double, toil and trouble
>
> Fire burn and cauldron bubble.

Prose is language that is not written in meter and that is much more irregular than verse in its rhythms. Prose tends to be akin to what is considered "normal" speech. History books, essays, articles, stories, and novels are mostly written in prose.

In the following passage, Benedick from *Much Ado About Nothing* speaks in prose about his desire to remain a bachelor:

> **BENEDICK:** That a woman conceived me, I thank her. That she brought me up, I likewise give her most humble thanks. Because I will not do them the wrong to mistrust any, I will do myself the right to trust none. I will live a bachelor.

Want to check if something is poetry or prose when reading Shakespeare? See if the first letter of each line is capitalized. If it is, then you are looking at poetry. If not, then you are looking at prose.

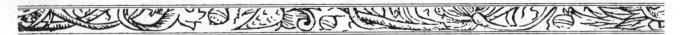

Iambic Pentameter
What's So Great About It Anyway?

Poets love how language sounds and they love to play with the rhythms of words. Meter is the steady rhythm that is created when syllables are stressed and unstressed in a systematic pattern. Of course, poets and playwrights have to arrange words in a certain order for a pattern to form.

Count the syllables of these lines:

> And pluck the wings from painted butterflies
> To fan the moonbeams from his sleeping eyes.
> — *A Midsummer Night's Dream*

There are ten in each, right? You have just read two lines of the most commonly used meter: iambic pentameter. *Iambic pentameter* is the meter most like natural speech, so it is perfect for a playwright such as Shakespeare.

Beat out on your chest this nonsense line of iambic pentameter:

> daDum daDum daDum daDum daDum

Now, beat out this line, which is also written in iambic pentameter:

> To fan the moonbeams from his sleeping eyes.

Iambic pentameter has ten syllables, like the lines above, and a regular rhythm. With iambic pentameter there are five feet of iambs.

- ◎ **A foot** is a metrical unit. One iamb is called a foot.

- ◎ **Pentameter** is a meterical line with five feet in it.

- ◎ **An iamb** is a metrical unit made up of two syllables, the first unstressed, the second stressed. "A dog" is an iamb.

- ◎ **Iambic pentameter** has 5 feet x 2 syllables = 10 syllables. *A dog in love will never be restrained* is an example of iambic pentameter.

Want to check if something is in iambic pentameter?

Count the syllables in each line. If there are ten syllables in each and the first word in each line is capitalized, then you are probably looking at iambic pentameter, but you should also check the stresses. Remember that the first word of each line in a poem is traditionally capitalized.

The Poetry Tool Kit

In these exercises, students explore the poetic devices simile, metaphor, personification, and alliteration.

On the Reproducible

Examples of similes, metaphors, personification, and alliteration

About the Exercise

Shakespeare's plays are rich in figurative language. To help students work with the imagery in his plays, review with them examples of poetic devices such as similes, metaphors, alliteration, and personification.

What to Do

Share with students the following descriptions of similes, metaphors, personification, and alliteration. Then, have students complete the examples on the reproducibles.

A simile is a comparison between two unlike objects that is connected by *like* or *as*. For example, "The sea was as quiet as a Sunday morning." A real thing—a calm sea—is described by comparing it to something essentially unlike it—in this case, a Sunday morning.

A metaphor occurs when two unlike things are compared to create an image. If we say, "The harvest moon is a great glowing Frisbee," then we are comparing the moon and a Frisbee to describe a certain kind of full moon. Or a line might read, "The great glowing Frisbee hovered over the night hikers."

With a **metaphor**, the comparison is often implied rather than stated. When we say, "That chicken avoided the fight," a coward is compared to a chicken, and the term *chicken* is used instead of the word *coward*.

Alliteration is a poetic device in which initial consonants are repeated. It makes the sound of language more striking. Here are some familiar alliterative pairs from everyday speech: rough and ready, bread and butter, safe and sound.

Personification occurs when a poet gives human qualities to something that is not human. An animal, object, or a concept is described using human terms. When a sportswriter writes "The sun deep-fried the baseball fans stuck on the bleachers," he personifies the sun, which cannot deep-fry something; only short-order cooks can do that.

Answers to the Reproducible

Part 1

Simile and Metaphor:

I will speak daggers to her but use none. [metaphor]

Methinks she hangs upon the cheek of night
Like a rich jewel in an Ethiop's ear. [simile]

'Tis not your inky brows, your black silk hair.
Your bugle eyeballs, nor your cheek of cream
That can entame my spirits to your worship.

[metaphor]

Part 2

Personification and Alliteration:

'Tis now the very witching time of night,
When churchyards yawn and hell itself breathes out
Contagion to this world: now could I drink hot
    blood,
And do such bitter business as the day
Would quake to look on.
Thus out of season, threading dark-eyed night

This happy breed of men, this little world
This precious stone set in the silver sea
I am never merry when I hear sweet music
The man that hath no music in himself
Nor is not mov'd with concord of sweet sounds,
Is fit for treasons, stratagems, and spoils;
The motions of his spirit are dull as night

Name _____ Date _____

The Poetry Tool Kit
Part 1: Simile and Metaphor

Imagery is poetic language that appeals to our senses and engages our imaginations; often it helps to create a strong visual image. Two devices that poets use to create strong visual images are similes and metaphors.

A simile is a comparison between two unlike objects that is connected by *like* or *as.*

A metaphor occurs when two essentially unlike things are compared to create an image. With a metaphor, the comparison often is implied rather than stated. When you say, "That chicken avoided the fight," the term *chicken* is used instead of the word *coward.*

Label the similes and the metaphors in the lines where you find them. What is the image they create? Is it a negative or positive image?

Methinks she hangs upon the cheek of night
Like a rich jewel in an Ethiop's ear
    (Romeo and Juliet)

I will speak daggers to her but use none.
    (Hamlet)

Love goes towards love as school boys from their books
But love from love towards school with heavy looks.
    (Romeo and Juliet)

Tis not your inky brows, your black silk hair.
Your bugle eyeballs, nor your cheek of cream
That can entame my spirits to your worship
    (As You Like It)

Note that a simile or metaphor can be revealing about character; in Romeo's line above, the comparison is especially fitting as both lovers are young and school-age. Juliet is only 14.

Now that you have looked at some metaphors and similes, practice writing with imagery. Finish the following phrases with an interesting comparison that creates a strong image:

Traveling home from school, when I am tired, I walk like a _____

Summer vacation is as welcome as _____

The backpack hung on her shoulders like _____

The taste of liver is like _____

That dirty old shoe looks like a _____

The Poetry Tool Kit
Part 2: Personification and Alliteration

Poets use many techniques to make their writing lively, interesting, and even musical. Personification and alliteration are two commonly used tools.

Personification occurs when a poet gives human qualities to something nonhuman, such as an animal, object, or concept.

The following passages contain at least three examples of personification. Can you find them?

'Tis now the very witching time of night,

When churchyards yawn and hell itself breathes out

Contagion to this world: now could I drink hot blood,   disease

And do such bitter business as the day

Would *quake* to look on.   tremble
    (Hamlet)

Thus out of season, threading dark-eyed night
    (King Lear)

Alliteration is a poetic device in which initial consonants are repeated. In the *Hamlet* passage above, Shakespeare uses alliteration when he says, "bitter business."

In the following passages, underline the places where alliteration occurs. Remember that words do not have to be right next to one another to alliterate.

This happy breed of men, this little world

This precious stone set in the silver sea
    (Richard II)

I am never merry when I hear sweet music

The man that hath no music in himself

Nor is not mov'd with concord of sweet sounds,

Is fit for treasons, stratagems, and spoils;

The motions of his spirit are dull as night
    (The Merchant of Venice)

Given the subject of the last passage (the importance of music), why might the poet want to emphasize *m*'s?

_____

_____

_____

Richard III
Determined to Be a Villain

On the Reproducible

Richard's opening soliloquy from act 1, scene 1 and a soliloquy from act 5, scene 3

Background

Richard III is one chapter of the War of the Roses that Shakespeare chronicled. The War of the Roses involved the struggle for the English throne between two royal families: the Lancasters, whose emblem was the red rose, and the Yorks, whose emblem was the white rose. These wars came to an end when Henry Tudor defeated Richard III at the Battle of Bosworth Field. Henry's ascension to the throne as Henry VII is considered by many scholars and historians to be the end of the Middle Ages.

These two speeches form a before-and-after picture of Richard III. In Richard's opening soliloquy, when he is not yet king, we see him explaining his dissatisfaction with peacetime. Richard, deformed since birth, believes he cannot be a lover, and therefore, announces his intention to be a villain. In the second speech, which comes late in the play and takes place on the eve of the Battle of Bosworth Field, we see Richard awakened by the ghosts of those he murdered on the way to the throne. He is faced with an aftershock he did not anticipate: "Coward" conscience comes to him.

Focal Points for Exploration

⊕ Reading Richard III's first speech provides students with a great opportunity to explore how character can be defined through a soliloquy in which the character's uncensored thoughts are expressed. Both speeches together allow students to consider how well a character knows himself. In the first speech, Richard does not anticipate how he will feel later.

⊕ Explore together how Richard's state of mind is reflected in the syntax. In the first speech, where Richard is more in control, his lines are more fluid and indicative of forethought. The second speech, on the other hand, is full of short lines and phrases and interruptions.

⊕ Note that Shakespeare makes extensive use of personification in both speeches, but especially the first. He refers, for example, to war as someone who "capers nimbly in a lady's chamber. ... " Ask students to find examples of personification in the first speech. (For more on personification, see The Poetry Tool Kit, page 25)

Discussion Questions for
"Now Is the Winter of Our Discontent"

1 What is the personified "war" doing now instead of mounting horses? *War has given up all of its usual activities and instead is absorbed in romantic nonsense ("merry meetings" and "sportive tricks").*

2 Interpret this line: "sent before my time/Into this breathing world." *The suggestion is that Richard was born prematurely, which caused his deformity and his present discomfort during days of peace and love.*

3 Why do dogs bark at him when he passes by? *Because he is so strange looking—lame and unfashionable.*

4 Why doesn't Richard think he can be a lover? *Because he looks so odd.*

5 What will he be instead of a lover? *A villain.*

Discussion Questions for
"Give Me Another Horse"

1. Why is Richard shouting for a horse? *He is dreaming of the battle he is to have the next day.*

2. What happens between the lines "Have mercy, Jesu!" and "*Soft!* I did but dream"? *He is coming out of his sleep and into the awareness that he was having a bad dream.*

3. Why do you think he calls his conscience coward? *Although Richard was able to commit all those murders, his conscience was horrified by it.*

4. How does Richard feel about himself? *Although Richard tries to overwhelm his conscience and convince himself that he does not care, in fact, he says, "I rather hate myself/For hateful deeds committed by myself!"*

Related Activities

Syntax & Sense:
An Acting Exercise

That Richard is generally in control and self-possessed in the first speech and, in the second, at the mercy of feelings he would rather ignore is reflected in the way he speaks. Shakespeare used different types of syntax and line lengths to create the effect of different states of mind.

Ask a good reader to read the first eight lines of the first speech while walking. The reader should change direction every time he or she hits a punctuation mark of any kind, including dashes. Then, have the same student read the first nine lines of the second speech the same way. This exercise, which is designed to help actors discover the emotional rhythms of the speech, is incredibly revealing. Ask students to make observations: Where does Richard seem more nervous? Where is he more in control? What is the quality and effect of the flowing lines in the first speech? What is the effect of all the broken lines and interruptions in the second speech? Ideally, all your students should have the experience of reading and feeling the difference between these two speeches. If you can take your students into a large

space and let all of them do the exercise, the effect can be quite wonderful (if somewhat chaotic).

A Divided Self

Split your class into two groups, and have the two groups stand in lines facing each other. Give each student a copy of the second speech. Have them read the speech aloud as two units. Group A reads the first line, Group B the second, Group A the third, and so on, until the end. I rather sternly warn them here that they need to stick together as they read; no voice should lag behind, rush ahead, or sound louder than the others.

By reading the speech in this way, students usually discover that Richard seems to have a divided self and that in this speech the two parts seem to be conversing with each other. If your class is too large to do this exercise easily, you can adapt it by having two students face each other and read alternating lines.

Impressions of Richard

Have students characterize and contrast Richard's state of mind in each speech in two tightly focused paragraphs. This assignment will work especially well if students have done the Syntax and Sense and A Divided Self activities. The first paragraph should probably be about the first speech, though you might ask students if there are any merits to beginning with the second speech. Remind them to use a strong topic sentence for each paragraph. Additionally, remind them that they will need to make a transition between paragraphs. Introduce them to good transitional words and phrases to use in contrasting paragraphs, such as "on the other hand" and "however."

Film Connection

Sir Laurence Olivier directed and acted the lead role in early film version of *Richard III.* A more recent version starred Ian McKellan as Richard III.

Richard III
Determined to Be a Villain, Part 1

Who's Who?

RICHARD, the duke of Gloucester of the York family, is the ambitious brother of the new king.

What's Happening?

War has recently ended. The House of York has defeated its enemy, the House of Lancaster. A period of peace and love is apparently at hand. Richard, who fought in the war and loved being a soldier, misses it already and longs to be king himself, not just brother of the king.

RICHARD: Now is the winter of our discontent	
Made glorious summer by this *son of York;*	the new king
And all the clouds that *lour'd* upon our house	lowered
In the deep bosom of the ocean buried.	
Grim-visaged war hath smooth'd his wrinkled *front;*	face
And now, instead of mounting *barbed* steeds	war-equipped
To fright the souls of fearful *adversaries,*	enemies
He capers nimbly in a lady's chamber	
To the lascivious pleasing of a lute.	
But I, that am not shaped for *sportive* tricks,	love games
Nor made to court an amorous looking-glass;	
I, that am rudely *stamp'd,* and *want* love's majesty	made/lack
To strut before a *wanton* ambling nymph;	morally loose
I, that am *curtail'd* of this fair proportion,	cut short
Cheated of feature by *dissembling* nature,	deceptive
Deformed, unfinish'd, sent before my time	
Into this breathing world, scarce half made up,	
And that so lamely and unfashionable	
That dogs bark at me as I halt by them;	
Why, I, in this weak piping time of peace,	
Have no delight to pass away the time,	
Unless to spy my shadow in the sun	
And *descant on* mine own deformity:	describe at length
And therefore, since I cannot prove a lover,	
To entertain these fair well-spoken days,	
I am determined to prove a villain.	

Irresistible Shakespeare Scholastic Professional Books

Richard III

Determined To Be a Villain, Part 2

Who's Who?

RICHARD, the duke of Gloucester, who has now become king of England.

What's Happening?

In order to become king, Richard has become responsible for many terrible, cruel deaths—his brothers, a wife, his nephews, several lords, and others. This speech takes place the midnight before the Battle of Bosworth Field. The next day Richard must fight his enemies, who wish to ovethrow him. Before this speech begins, the ghosts of his victims have come to Richard in the night to curse his defense of the throne.

KING RICHARD III: Give me another horse: bind up my wounds.
Have mercy, Jesu!—*Soft!* I did but dream.   Quiet
O coward conscience, how dost thou afflict me!
The lights burn blue. It is now dead midnight.
Cold fearful drops stand on my trembling flesh.
What do I fear? Myself? There's none else by:
Richard loves Richard; that is, I am I.
Is there a murderer here? No. Yes, I am:
Then fly. What, from myself? Great reason why:
Lest I revenge. What, myself upon myself? in case
Alack. I love myself. Wherefore? for any good
That I myself have done unto myself?
O, no! Alas, I rather hate myself
For hateful deeds committed by myself!
I am a villain: yet I lie. I am not.
Fool, of thyself speak well: fool, do not flatter.
My conscience hath a thousand several tongues,
And every tongue brings in a several tale,
And every tale condemns me for a villain.
Perjury, perjury, in the high'st degree false testimony
Murder, stern murder, in the *direst* degree; most dreadful
All several sins, all used in each degree,
Throng to the bar, crying all, Guilty! guilty!
I shall despair. There is no creature loves me;
And if I die, no soul shall pity me:
Nay, wherefore should they, since that I myself
Find in myself no pity to myself?
Methought the souls of all that I had murder'd
Came to my tent; and every one did threat
Tomorrow's vengeance on the head of Richard.

Henry V
This Story Shall the Good Man Teach His Son

On the Reproducible

A scene adapted from act 4, scene 3 of *Henry V*

Background

Henry V, based on *Holinshed's Chronicles,* is perhaps Shakespeare's most popular history play. In the play, Shakespeare explores the characteristics of the ideal ruler for England. In *Henry IV, Part One,* Henry V is a fun-loving prince, nicknamed Hal, who has a reputation for drinking, dancing, stealing, and generally shirking his duties. In some ways the young Henry V develops this reputation to put men off guard, so that when he does become king, he will shine all the brighter when he shows the discipline, leadership, and courage of which he is capable.

Henry V opens with the English contemplating war against France to regain lands thought to belong to England not France. In the midst of this controversy a French ambassador arrives with an insulting message from the King of France's son, the Dauphin. Referring to the King's "wilder days" as a prince, the message states that there is nothing that can be won in France with a dance. Through the ambassador the Dauphin asks to hear no more about the lands in question and sends a gift befitting Henry's frivolous nature: tennis balls. Henry responds icily: "We are glad the Dauphin is so pleasant with us." This fresh insult takes the political conflict and makes it personal. King Henry promptly declares war against France.

The scene presented here comes in the fourth act of the play, moments before the decisive battle on the fields of Agincourt.

Focal Points for Exploration

- The St. Crispin's Day speech is a masterpiece of persuasion. Ask students to look closely at how King Henry persuades his men and changes their mood. What techniques does he use? The general emotional appeal of the speech, you might remind them, could be used for good or evil purposes.

- In addition to tracking the intentions of the king, ask students to look closely at Westmoreland and the role he plays in the scene. How he feels before and after the speech provides an indication of the power and effectiveness of the speech.

Discussion Questions

1 Why does Westmoreland wish for more men? *Because they are outnumbered five to one and the French troops are fresh.*

2 What does King Henry mean when he says, "The fewer men, the greater share of honour"? *That if they win with as few men as they have, they will have all the more honor.*

3 Why does Henry V say he will let leave whomever doesn't want to fight? How is he trying to make the men feel? *By saying that they can leave, the king gives his troops a sense of choice and a feeling of personal pride in what they are doing. His intention, however, is to persuade his men to stay. He subtly implies that anyone who would leave because he has "no stomach to this fight" is a coward.*

4 What is the effect when he says, "We few, we happy few." How does he make the men feel about fighting together? *He turns their short numbers into an advantage by creating a sense of intimacy about their fighting unit. He envisions them as a band of brothers.*

5 Overall, what is the intention of his speech? *To highlight the valor of the fighting men, bond them together, and steel them to the task of fighting the vast French troops.*

6 How does Westmoreland feel after he hears this speech? *Inspired by the king, he wishes there were even fewer men.*

Related Activities

The Power of Persuasion

Ask students to write an analysis of Henry's persuasive powers in the St. Crispin's Day speech. How does Henry persuade his tired men to want to fight? What are the specific words, phrases, and images that would make men fight when the odds are against them? What techniques does he use? Depending on your students, this could simply be a paragraph or a complete essay.

"Rather Proclaim It..."
A Memorization Activity

Consider having students memorize some of the St. Crispin's Day speech. They could learn a longer stretch of it, from the lines "Rather proclaim it, Westmoreland, through my host" to the end of the speech. Or they could learn just a handful of lines, from "This story shall the good man teach his son" to the end of the speech.

Film Connection

A wonderful follow-up to reading, interpreting, and acting out this scene is to watch Kenneth Branagh's version of *Henry V*. (If you are pressed for time, you could show only this scene from the film.) Once students have studied this scene in depth, they will be in a fine position to see the film. It is useful for students to have time to explore the scene on their own before seeing the film. Then they will view the film as an interpretation of the text, which will help build critical thinking and interpretive skills.

Henry V
This Story Shall the Good Man Teach His Son

Who's Who?

HENRY V, king of England

DUKES OF GLOUCESTER and BEDFORD, the king's brothers

DUKE OF EXETER, the uncle of the king

SALISBURY and WESTMORELAND, English earls, cousins of the king

SIR THOMAS ERPINGHAM, a lord

MONTJOY, the French herald

What's Happening?

Tired English troops, who have been on a long military campaign in France during the Hundred Years War, are about to face a battle against the French troops on the fields of Agincourt. The French are not only "fresh," that is well rested and well equipped, but they outnumber the English five to one. As the scene opens, the king's leading men voice doubt about their prospects in battle. At first King Henry is not present.

The English camp

Enter GLOUCESTER, BEDFORD, EXETER, ERPINGHAM, with all his host: SALISBURY and WESTMORELAND

GLOUCESTER: Where is the king?

BEDFORD: The king himself is rode to view their *battle*.   army

WESTMORELAND: Of fighting men they have full *three score thousand*.   60,000

EXETER: There's five to one; besides, they all are fresh.

SALISBURY: God's arm strike with us! 'Tis a fearful odds.
God be wi' you, princes all; I'll to my *charge:*   fighting post
If we no more meet till we meet in heaven,
Then, joyfully, my noble Lord of Bedford,
My dear Lord Gloucester, and my good
  Lord Exeter,
And my kind kinsman, warriors all, *adieu!*   good-bye

Irresistible Shakespeare Scholastic Professional Books

BEDFORD: Farewell, good Salisbury; and good luck go with thee!

EXETER: Farewell, kind lord; fight valiantly today:
And yet I do thee wrong to *mind* thee of it,   remind
For thou art framed of the firm truth of *valour*.   bravery

[Exit SALISBURY]

BEDFORD: He is full of valour as of kindness;
Princely in both.

[Enter the KING]

WESTMORELAND: O that we now had here
But one ten thousand of those men in England
That do no work today!

KING HENRY V: What's he that wishes so?
My cousin Westmoreland? No, my fair cousin:
If we are mark'd to die, we are *enow*   enough
To do our country loss; and if to live,
The fewer men, the greater share of honour.
God's will! I pray thee, wish not one man more.
By Jove, I am not *covetous* for gold,   desirous
Nor care I who doth feed upon my cost;
It *earns me not* if men my garments wear;   doesn't matter
Such outward things dwell not in my desires:
But if it be a sin to covet honour,
I am the most offending soul alive.
No, faith, my *coz*, wish not a man from England: cousin
God's peace! I would not lose so great an honour
As one man more, methinks, would share from me
For the best hope I have. O, do not wish one more!
Rather proclaim it, Westmoreland, through my *host*,   army
That he which hath no *stomach* to this fight,   appetite for
Let him depart; his passport shall be made
And *crowns for convoy* put into his purse: travel funds
We would not die in that man's company
That fears his fellowship to die with us.
This day is called the feast of Crispian:
He that outlives this day, and comes safe home,
Will stand a tip-toe when the day is named,
And rouse him at the name of Crispian.
He that shall see this day, and live old age,
Will yearly on the vigil feast his neighbours,
And say 'To-morrow is Saint Crispian:'
Then will he strip his sleeve and show his scars.
And say 'These wounds I had on Crispin's day.'
Old men forget: yet all shall be forgot,
But he'll remember with advantages
What feats he did that day: then shall our names.
Familiar in his mouth as household words

Harry the king, Bedford and Exeter,
Warwick and Talbot, Salisbury and Gloucester,
Be in their flowing cups freshly remember'd.
This story shall the good man teach his son;
And Crispin Crispian shall ne'er go by,
From this day to the ending of the world,
But we in it shall be remembered;
We few, we happy few, we band of brothers;
For he today that sheds his blood with me
Shall be my brother; be he ne'er so *vile*,   low born
This day shall *gentle his condition:*   make him a gentleman
And gentlemen in England now a-bed
Shall think themselves accursed they were not here,
And hold their manhoods cheap whiles any speaks
That fought with us upon Saint Crispin's day.

[*Re-enter SALISBURY*]

SALISBURY: My sovereign lord, *bestow yourself* with speed: take your position
The French are bravely in their *battles* set,   battle lines
And will with all *expedience* charge on us.   speed

KING HENRY V: All things are ready, if our minds be so.

WESTMORELAND: Perish the man whose mind is backward now!

KING HENRY V: Thou dost not wish more help from England, coz?

WESTMORELAND: God's will! my liege, would you and I alone,
Without more help, could fight this royal battle!

KING HENRY V: Why, now thou hast *unwish'd* five thousand men;   wished away
Which likes me better than to wish us one.
You know your places: God be with you all!

[*Tucket. Enter MONTJOY*]   trumpet fanfare

MONTJOY: Once more I come to know of thee, King Harry,
If for thy ransom thou wilt now *compound*,   arrange
Before thy most assured overthrow.

KING HENRY V: Who hath sent thee now?

MONTJOY: The Constable of France.

KING HENRY V: I pray thee, bear my former answer back:
Bid them *achieve me* and then sell my bones.   get me
Good God! why should they mock poor fellows thus?
Let me speak proudly: tell the constable
We are but warriors for the working-day;
Our gayness and our gilt are all *besmirch'd*   soiled
With rainy marching in the painful field;
There's not a piece of feather in our host—
Good argument, I hope, we will not fly—
And time hath worn us into *slovenry:*   filth
But, by the mass, our hearts are *in the trim;*   in excellent shape

Irresistible Shakespeare Scholastic Professional Books

And my poor soldiers tell me, yet ere night
They'll be in fresher robes, or they will pluck
The gay new coats o'er the French soldiers' heads
And turn them out of service. If they do this,—
As, if God please, they shall,—my ransom then
Will soon be levied. Herald, save thou thy labour;
Come thou no more for ransom, gentle herald:
They shall have none, I swear, but these my joints;
Which if they have as I will leave 'em them,
Shall yield them little, tell the constable.

MONTJOY: I shall, King Harry. And so fare thee well:
Thou never shalt hear herald any more.

[Exit]

KING HENRY V: I fear thou'lt once more come again for ransom.

[Enter YORK]

YORK: My lord, most humbly on my knee I beg
The leading of the *vanguard*.   foremost troops

KING HENRY V: Take it, brave York. Now, soldiers, march away:
And how thou pleasest, God, *dispose* the day!   decide

[Exit]

As You Like It
We Have Seen Better Days

On the Reproducible

A scene adapted from act 2, scenes 1, 6, and 7 of *As You Like It*

Background

The characters in *As You Like It* are restored from the corrupt influences of civilization by an experience in nature. They go into the Forest of Arden and there rediscover what life is about. In act 1, we see ample evidence of the corrupt life of the court in the bad and selfish behavior of both Oliver (Orlando's brother) and Duke Ferdinand (Duke Senior's brother). The two bad brothers exile the two good brothers, Orlando and Duke Senior, to the woods. Another character whom we do not meet in this scene is Rosalind, Duke Senior's daughter (who is newly in love with Orlando).

Focal Points for Exploration

◉ Explore with students how a visit to nature, away from corrupt civilization (here the court), might be a cause of spiritual and personal renewal. By the end of the play, the bad brothers have also been to the Forest of Arden and experienced a conversion to better ways.

◉ In the midst of this play is the cynic Jaques, who describes men and women as "merely players" in the famous "All the world's a stage" speech. Have students think about why Shakespeare might have put him in the play. Ask them to imagine the scene here presented without him.

◉ You have a good opportunity here to generate some discussion about why Adam and Orlando's opening lines are in prose and the rest is in poetry. Ask students to speculate after they have read the scene.

◉ You might also explain to students that motley is the traditional clothing of fools. Fools were often part of a proper court. They told jokes, were fond of puns, and were uniquely licensed to say whatever they wanted to great men.

Discussion Questions

1 Why do you think Duke Senior is going to such lengths to explain why it is good to live in the woods? How do you suspect his attendant lords are feeling? *They are probably tired and sick of roughing it because they are used to life at court.*

2 Why does Adam lie down at the beginning of the scene? *He is too weak to go on without food.*

3 Fools can criticize as they please. Why do you think Jaques wants to be a fool? *Like a fool, he wants to be able to say what he pleases about whomever he wants. By pointing out others, mistakes and failings, he will "cleanse the foul body of the infected world."*

4 Why does Duke Senior tell Orlando "Your gentleness shall force/More than your force move us to gentleness"? *Orlando has drawn his sword upon the feeding men before asking. He assumes that because he is in the forest, he must act savagely to get what he needs.*

5 In Jaques's famous "All the world's a stage" speech, he says men and women are merely players. What is his attitude toward human beings? How noble and grand do they appear in his speech? *His attitude seems to reduce human beings to players—actors rather than individuals making reasonable choices. In general his examples of the stages of man make people sound pathetic.*

Related Activities

Acting It Out

This is a wonderful scene for students to act out. Through the process of figuring out what is happening, students will naturally have to read very carefully and critically. Begin by asking students to read the scene through carefully to make sure they understand it before acting it out. Ask for volunteers to be the acting guinea pigs, and have the rest of the class work together to direct the scene. Group direction can be unruly, so you might try to collect everyone's ideas and then summarize them or choose the most interesting ones to try out.

As you study the scene, have students try to figure out what is happening on stage. For example, when Orlando is first helping the failing Adam, what action is happening as he speaks?

An Acting Exercise

To get students to think creatively about what is happening at the beginning of the scene, ask them to act it out as if the Duke were wearing a great big coat and Amiens a little shred of clothing. Have the other students create wind noises. Ask students what it might suggest about the Duke if the scene were played this way. Is he more adapted to the woods simply because he is more comfortable and unaware of the others' discomfort? Then, ask students to act it out again, this time with the Duke giving his coat to a shivering Amiens halfway through. Ask them to discuss how these directions change what the scene means.

Memorize It: "All the World's a Stage"

Have students commit to memory the first four lines of Jaques's famous "All the world's a stage" speech. If they are interested, students might try to memorize a longer passage.

An Expository Paragraph

Have students respond to the following in a paragraph with a strong topic sentence:

> What is Jaques's attitude toward human beings in his "All the world's a stage" speech? Does he speak fondly of the stages of life?

To get students started, ask them to discuss how he characterizes infancy, a time of life we view with nearly universal affection. Jaques, however, speaks of babies "mewling and puking." Tell students that as they write their paragraphs they should refer to specifc lines. They can do this by quoting a word or two or the line in its entirety. You might share the following examples with them:

> *Jaques speaks with horror of the "mewling and puking" of infants.*

> *Jaques has nothing good to say about man, even in his earliest days: "At first the infant/Mewling and puking in the nurse's arms."*

Explain to students that lines of poetry are set off by slashes when they are being quoted in this manner.

"His Acts Being Seven Stages"

After students are familiar with Jaques's speech, have them write a speech that depicts their own view of the stages of man. Encourage them to come up with a strong point of view for the phases of life. They might also try to write from the point of view of an imaginary character such as a fairy-tale creation like Cinderella or a character from a favorite novel or movie.

A Picture of Arden

The Forest of Arden is an important part of *As You Like It*. Ask students to write a descriptive paragraph about what they think Arden is like. How do they imagine the forest? What sense of the place do they get from the play? How do the characters describe it? Let them know that, by the end of the play, the forest has had a positive effect on its visitors, improving their lives.

As You Like It
We Have Seen Better Days

Who's Who?

DUKE SENIOR, a good and kind duke exiled by a cruel brother (he has a
daughter of marrying age)

AMIENS, a lord attendant upon the Duke

JAQUES, a bored but loyal lord, also attendant upon the Duke

ORLANDO, a young nobleman, fleeing a cruel brother (he is of marrying age)

ADAM, his faithful, elderly family servant

What's Happening?

At first this scene switches back and forth between different sets of characters who
have recently had to flee life at court to rough it in the Forest of Arden. Both Orlando
and Duke Senior, who meet for the first time in the following scene, have violently
jealous brothers who forced them to leave home. They must now survive in the forest.

As the scene opens, Duke Senior is trying to describe the up-side of exile in the
forest to his loyal lords. Soon after we meet Orlando and Adam, who are newly in the
forest and looking unsuccessfully for food.

The Forest of Arden

Enter DUKE SENIOR, AMIENS, and two or three Lords, like foresters

DUKE SENIOR: Now, my comates and brothers in exile,
Hath not old custom made this life more sweet
Than that of painted *pomp*? Are not these woods   splendor
More free from peril than the envious court?
Here feel we but the penalty of Adam,
The seasons' difference, as the icy fang
And churlish *chiding* of the winter's wind,   scolding
Which, when it bites and blows upon my body,
Even till I shrink with cold, I smile and say
'This is no flattery: these are counsellors
That feelingly persuade me what I am.'
Sweet are the uses of adversity.
And this our life exempt from public haunt
Finds tongues in trees, books in the running brooks,
Sermons in stones and good in everything.
I would not change it.

AMIENS: Happy is your grace,
That can translate the stubbornness of fortune
Into so quiet and so sweet a style.   *[They exit]*

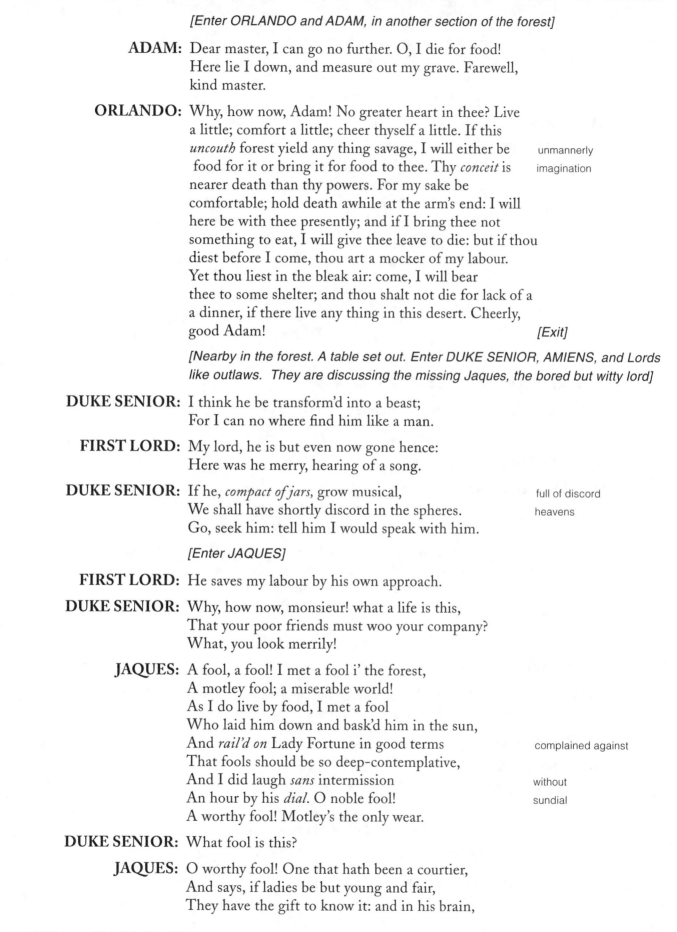

[Enter ORLANDO and ADAM, in another section of the forest]

ADAM: Dear master, I can go no further. O, I die for food!
Here lie I down, and measure out my grave. Farewell,
kind master.

ORLANDO: Why, how now, Adam! No greater heart in thee? Live
a little; comfort a little; cheer thyself a little. If this
uncouth forest yield any thing savage, I will either be   unmannerly
food for it or bring it for food to thee. Thy *conceit* is   imagination
nearer death than thy powers. For my sake be
comfortable; hold death awhile at the arm's end: I will
here be with thee presently; and if I bring thee not
something to eat, I will give thee leave to die: but if thou
diest before I come, thou art a mocker of my labour.
Yet thou liest in the bleak air: come, I will bear
thee to some shelter; and thou shalt not die for lack of a
a dinner, if there live any thing in this desert. Cheerly,
good Adam!   [Exit]

[Nearby in the forest. A table set out. Enter DUKE SENIOR, AMIENS, and Lords
like outlaws. They are discussing the missing Jaques, the bored but witty lord]

DUKE SENIOR: I think he be transform'd into a beast;
For I can no where find him like a man.

FIRST LORD: My lord, he is but even now gone hence:
Here was he merry, hearing of a song.

DUKE SENIOR: If he, *compact of jars*, grow musical,   full of discord
We shall have shortly discord in the spheres.   heavens
Go, seek him: tell him I would speak with him.

[Enter JAQUES]

FIRST LORD: He saves my labour by his own approach.

DUKE SENIOR: Why, how now, monsieur! what a life is this,
That your poor friends must woo your company?
What, you look merrily!

JAQUES: A fool, a fool! I met a fool i' the forest,
A motley fool; a miserable world!
As I do live by food, I met a fool
Who laid him down and bask'd him in the sun,
And *rail'd on* Lady Fortune in good terms   complained against
That fools should be so deep-contemplative,
And I did laugh *sans* intermission   without
An hour by his *dial*. O noble fool!   sundial
A worthy fool! Motley's the only wear.

DUKE SENIOR: What fool is this?

JAQUES: O worthy fool! One that hath been a courtier,
And says, if ladies be but young and fair,
They have the gift to know it: and in his brain,

Which is as dry as the remainder biscuit
After a voyage, he hath strange places cramm'd
With observation, the which he vents
In mangled forms. O that I were a fool!
I am ambitious for a motley coat.

DUKE SENIOR: Thou shalt have one.

JAQUES: It is my only suit;
Provided that you weed your better judgments
Of all opinion that grows rank in them
That I am wise. I must have liberty
Withal, as large a charter as the wind,
To *blow on* whom I please; for so fools have.   criticize
Invest me in my motley; give me leave
To speak my mind, and I will through and through
Cleanse the foul body of the infected world,
If they will patiently receive my medicine
But who comes here?

[Enter ORLANDO, with his sword drawn]

ORLANDO: *Forbear*, and eat no more.   refrain, stop

JAQUES: Why, I have eat none yet.

ORLANDO: Nor shalt not, till necessity be served.

JAQUES: Of what kind should this cock come of?

DUKE SENIOR: Art thou thus *bolden'd*, man, by thy distress,   made bold
Or else a rude despiser of good manners,
That in civility thou seem'st so empty?

ORLANDO: You touch'd my *vein* at first: the thorny point   condition
Of bare distress hath *ta'en* from me the show   taken
Of smooth civility: yet am I inland bred
And know some nurture. But forbear, I say:
He dies that touches any of this fruit
Till I and my affairs are answered.

JAQUES: *An* you will not be answered with reason, I must die.   If

DUKE SENIOR: What would you have? Your gentleness shall force
More than your force move us to gentleness.

ORLANDO: I almost die for food; and let me have it.

DUKE SENIOR: Sit down and feed, and welcome to our table.

ORLANDO: Speak you so gently? Pardon me, I pray you:
I thought that all things had been savage here;
And therefore put I on the *countenance*   behavior
Of stern commandment. But whate'er you are
That in this desert inaccessible,
Under the shade of melancholy boughs,
Lose and neglect the creeping hours of time

If ever you have look'd on better days,
If ever been where bells have knoll'd to church,
If ever sat at any good man's feast,
If ever from your eyelids wiped a tear
And know what 'tis to pity and be pitied,
Let gentleness my strong enforcement be:
In the which hope I blush, and hide my sword.

DUKE SENIOR: True is it that we have seen better days,
And have with holy bell been *knoll'd* to church   rung
And sat at good men's feasts and wiped our eyes
Of drops that sacred pity hath *engender'd:*   caused
And therefore sit you down in gentleness
And take upon command what help we have
That to your wanting may be minister'd.

ORLANDO: Then but forbear your food a little while,
Whiles, like a doe, I go to find my fawn
And give it food. There is an old poor man,
Who after me hath many a weary step
Limp'd in pure love: till he be first sufficed,
Oppress'd with two weak evils, age and hunger,
I will not touch a bit.

DUKE SENIOR: Go find him out,
And we will nothing *waste* till you return.   use up

ORLANDO: I thank ye; and be blest for your good comfort!

[Exit]

DUKE SENIOR: Thou see'st we are not all alone unhappy:
This wide and universal theatre
Presents more woeful pageants than the scene
Wherein we play in.

JAQUES: All the world's a stage,
And all the men and women merely players:
They have their exits and their entrances;
And one man in his time plays many parts,
His acts being seven ages. At first the infant,
Mewling and puking in the nurse's arms.   crying meekly
And then the whining school-boy, with his satchel
And shining morning face, creeping like snail
Unwillingly to school. And then the lover,
Sighing like furnace, with a woeful ballad
Made to his mistress' eyebrow. Then a soldier,
Full of strange oaths and bearded like the *pard,*   panther
Jealous in honour, sudden and quick in quarrel,
Seeking the bubble reputation
Even in the cannon's mouth. And then the justice,
In fair round belly with good capon lined,
With eyes severe and beard of formal cut,

Full of wise *saws* and modern instances;   sayings
And so he plays his part. The sixth age shifts
Into the lean and slipper'd *pantaloon*,   foolish old man
With spectacles on nose and pouch on side,
His youthful hose, well saved, a world too wide
For his shrunk shank; and his big manly voice,
Turning again toward childish treble, pipes
And whistles in his sound. Last scene of all,
That ends this strange eventful history,
Is second childishness and mere oblivion,
Sans teeth, sans eyes, sans taste, sans everything.   without

[Re-enter ORLANDO, with ADAM]

DUKE SENIOR: Welcome. Set down your venerable *burthen*,   burden
And let him feed.

ORLANDO: I thank you most for him.

ADAM: So had you need:
I scarce can speak to thank you for myself.

DUKE SENIOR: Welcome; fall to: I will not trouble you
As yet, to question you about your fortunes.
Give us some music; and, good cousin, sing.

[Song]

AMIENS: Blow, blow, thou winter wind.
Thou art not so unkind
As man's ingratitude;
Thy tooth is not so keen,
Because thou art not seen,
Although thy breath be rude.
Heigh-ho! sing, heigh-ho! unto the green holly:
Most friendship is feigning, most loving mere folly:
Then, heigh-ho, the holly!
This life is most jolly.
Freeze, freeze, thou bitter sky,
That dost not bite so nigh
As benefits forgot:
Though thou the waters warp,
Thy sting is not so sharp
As friend remember'd not.
Heigh-ho! sing, & c.

DUKE SENIOR: Good old man,
Thou art right welcome as thy master is.
Support him by the arm. Give me your hand,
And let me all your fortunes understand.

The Taming of the Shrew
Am I Not Christopher Sly?

On the Reproducible

A scene adapted from the Induction of *The Taming of the Shrew*

Background

The Taming of the Shrew opens with the Induction, a scene in which a rich, arrogant lord plays a joke on a man of undistinguished birth, the beggar Christopher Sly. The lord takes Sly, whom he finds passed out cold from drink, and removes him to his home, where he sets up an elaborate deception. The lord, together with his friends and servants, attempts to fool Sly into believing he is actually a lord who has been in a bad dream for 15-odd years (in this dream he is the beggar Sly). How successful the lord is in his rouse is a matter of interpretation.

This scene works as a frame for the famous story of Katherine and Petruchio. As the Induction comes to an end, Sly sits down with his "wife" (a part played by a page to the lord) to watch some players perform a play, which is *The Taming of the Shrew. Shrew* is a play within a play.

Focal Points for Exploration

⊚ The class dynamics presented in this scene are worth exploring. An arrogant lord, apparently in need of constant entertainment, plays with, or as he says, "practices on," the life of another man. The lord and the beggar are opposites in terms of social position, and the lord treats Sly as an object to be manipulated for his amusement. He does not treat his page much better, insisting that he dress in women's clothing and pretend to be Sly's wife. One could easily argue, however, that a time comes in the scene when Sly begins to understand what is happening, therefore turning the tables on the lord.

⊚ Practical jokes are poised between cruelty and merriment. In reading this scene and in acting it out, students can explore and attempt to define its tone. Is the scene lighthearted or are there elements of cruelty in how the lord behaves?

⊚ Prose and poetry are both used in this scene. Ask students to explore how each is employed, especially at the end of the scene, where Sly moves between poetry and prose.

Discussion Questions

1 Why does the Hostess ask Sly if he will not pay for the glasses he has burst? Why did he break the glasses? *Because he has been drunk and disorderly inside her ale house.*

2 What is the lord's attitude toward Sly when he finds him, and what words and phrases best demonstrate it? *The lord looks at Sly disdainfully and from his first words describes him as subhuman, referring to him as a "beast" and as a "swine" who is "foul and loathsome."*

3 What sort of man is the lord? What kind of life does he lead? *The lord appears to spend his time in common aristocratic activities, such as hunting and hawking, and he clearly has time enough for idle pursuits, such as deceiving Christopher Sly.*

Related Activities

Acting It Out

This scene is a wonderful one for students to act out; it can be absolutely hilarious. Have them work to discover and create as much comedy as they can. They should easily grasp the more obvious moments, such as the easy humor of the comically drunk man, but help them to envision the significance of other moments as well, such as when the page, dressed as a woman, sits alongside Sly, who immediately suggests they go to bed.

At the same time, this is not simple slapstick. There is a potentially dark edge to this comedy, for example, when a bored lord makes sport with another man's sense of reality. Ask students to think carefully about who should be more likable for the audience, the lord or Sly.

A Plot With a Practical Joke

Ask students to write a story that revolves around a practical joke. Their stories might include the buildup to the joke, the joke itself, and the aftermath of the joke. In addition to thinking of some prank for their story, they will also need to think of the characters and their motivations. Who plays the joke and why? What is the relationship between the joker and his victim?

A Conversation Between Classes: A Dramatic Writing Activity

Have students write a scene in which an upper-class and a lower-class person find themselves in a situation together in which they have to converse with each other. Perhaps they are stuck together on a train, or waiting on line somewhere. Perhaps they argue, or perhaps their conversation leads them to believe that all human beings have essentially the same kinds of problems. Tell students to pay close attention to the language they use for each character; we should be able to tell which character is which, even without the speaker tags. Before they get started, show students how to set up dialogue on the page, and explain that they should print the character's name in capital letters.

The Taming of the Shrew
Am I Not Christopher Sly?

Who's Who?

CHRISTOPHER SLY, a beggar

HOSTESS, of an ale house

THE LORD, a rich young man, fond of hunting and games

FIRST HUNTSMAN

SECOND HUNTSMAN

PAGE, to the lord

What's Happening?

The following scene is the opening to *The Taming of the Shrew*. Here, a drunk beggar, on the verge of collapse outside a bar, argues with the hostess about his unpaid bill.

Before an ale house on a heath.

Enter Hostess and SLY

SLY: I'll *feeze you*, in faith.   get you

HOSTESS: A pair of stocks, you *rogue*!   tramp

SLY: You're a baggage! The Slys are no rogues. Look in
the chronicles—we came in with Richard Conqueror.
Therefore *paucas pallabris:* let the world slide. *Sessa*!   few words/quiet

HOSTESS: You will not pay for the glasses you have burst?

SLY: No, not a *denier*. Go by, Saint Jeronimy! Go to thy   small coin
cold bed, and warm thee.

HOSTESS: I know my remedy, I must go fetch the *thirdborough*.   constable

[Exit]

SLY: Third, or fourth, or fifth borough, I'll answer him
by the law: I'll not budge an inch, boy: let him come,
and kindly.

[Falls asleep]

[Horns winded. Enter a Lord from hunting, with his dogs and huntsmen]

LORD: Huntsman, I charge thee, *tender* well my hounds: care for
Breathe Merriman, the poor *cur* is *emboss'd*;   mongrel/exhausted
And couple Clowder with the deep-mouth'd *brach*.   hunting bitch
Saw'st thou not, boy, how Silver made it good
At the hedge-corner, *in the coldest fault*?   when the scent was lost
I would not lose the dog for twenty pound.

FIRST HUNTSMAN: Why, Belman is as good as he, my lord.
And twice to-day pick'd out the dullest scent:
Trust me, I take him for the better dog.

LORD: Thou art a fool: if Echo were as *fleet*,   swift
I would esteem him worth a dozen such.
But sup them well and look unto them all:
Tomorrow I intend to hunt again.

FIRST HUNTSMAN: I will, my lord.

LORD: What's here? One dead, or drunk? See, doth he breathe?

SECOND HUNTSMAN: He breathes, my lord. Were he not warm'd with ale,
This were a bed but cold to sleep so soundly.

LORD: O monstrous beast! how like a swine he lies!
Grim death, how foul and loathsome is thine image!
Sirs, I will *practise* on this drunken man.   play a trick
What think you, if he were convey'd to bed,
Wrapp'd in sweet clothes, rings put upon his fingers,
A most delicious banquet by his bed,
And brave attendants near him when he wakes,
Would not the beggar then forget himself?

FIRST HUNTSMAN: Believe me, lord, I think he cannot choose.

SECOND HUNTSMAN: It would seem strange unto him when he waked.

LORD: Even as a flattering dream or worthless fancy.
Then take him up and manage well the jest:
Carry him gently to my fairest chamber
And hang it round with all my wanton pictures:
Balm his foul head in warm distilled waters
And burn sweet wood to make the lodging sweet:
Procure me music ready when he wakes,
To make a *dulcet* and a heavenly sound;   melodious
And if he chance to speak, be ready straight
And with a low *submissive* reverence   humbly obedient
Say 'What is it your honour will command?'
Let one attend him with a silver basin
Full of rose-water and bestrew'd with flowers,
Another bear the ewer, the third a *diaper*,   towel
And say 'Will't please your lordship cool your hands?'
Some one be ready with a costly suit
And ask him what apparel he will wear;
Another tell him of his hounds and horse,
And that his lady mourns at his disease:

Persuade him that he hath been lunatic;
And when he says he is, say that he dreams,
For he is nothing but a mighty lord.
This do and do it kindly, gentle sirs:
It will be pastime passing excellent,
If it be *husbanded with modesty*.   done with restraint

FIRST HUNTSMAN: My lord, I warrant you we will play our part,
As he shall think by our true diligence
He is no less than what we say he is.

LORD: Take him up gently and to bed with him;
And each one to his office when he wakes.

[Some bear out SLY]

Sirrah, go you to Barthol'mew my page,
And see him dress'd in all suits like a lady:
That done, conduct him to the drunkard's chamber;
And call him 'madam,' *do him obeisance*.   pay him great respect
Tell him from me, as he will win my love,
He bear himself with honourable action,
Such as he hath observed in noble ladies
Unto their lords, by them accomplished:
Such duty to the drunkard let him do
With soft low tongue and lowly courtesy,
And say 'What is't your honour will command,
Wherein your lady and your humble wife
May show her duty and make known her love?'
And then with kind embracements, tempting kisses,
And with declining head into his bosom,
Bid him shed tears, as being overjoy'd
To see her noble lord restored to health,
Who for this seven years hath *esteem'd him*   believed him
No better than a poor and loathsome beggar:
And if the boy have not a woman's gift
To rain a shower of commanded tears,
An onion will do well for such a *shift*,   act, trick
Which in a napkin being close convey'd
Shall in despite enforce a watery eye.
See this dispatch'd with all the haste thou canst:
Anon I'll give thee more instructions.

[Exit a Servingman]

I know the boy will well *usurp* the grace,   assume
Voice, gait and action of a gentlewoman:
I long to hear him call the drunkard husband.

[Exit]

[A bedchamber in the Lord's house.]

*[Enter aloft SLY, with Attendants; some with apparel, others with basin and ewer
and appurtenances; and Lord]*

SLY:	For God's sake, a pot of small *ale*.	cheap beer
FIRST SERVANT:	Will't please your lordship drink a cup of *sack*?	sherry
SECOND SERVANT:	Will't please your honour taste of these *conserves*?	candied fruit
THIRD SERVANT:	What *raiment* will your honour wear to-day?	clothing

SLY: I am Christopher Sly; call not me 'honour' nor
'lordship:' I ne'er drank sack in my life; and if
you give me any conserves, give me conserves of
beef: ne'er ask me what raiment I'll wear; for I
have no more *doublets* than backs, no more stockings   jackets
than legs, nor no more shoes than feet; nay,
sometimes more feet than shoes, or such shoes as my
toes look through the over-leather.

LORD: Heaven cease this idle *humour* in your honour!   fantasy
O, that a mighty man of such descent,
Of such possessions and so high esteem,
Should be infused with so foul a spirit!

SLY: What, would you make me mad? Am not I Christopher
Sly, old Sly's son of Burtonheath, by birth a
pedlar, by education a cardmaker, by transmutation a
bear-herd, and now by present profession a *tinker*?   mender of pots

THIRD SERVANT: O, this it is that makes your lady mourn!

SECOND SERVANT: O, this is it that makes your servants droop!

LORD: Hence comes it that your *kindred* shuns your house,   family
As beaten hence by your strange lunacy.
O noble lord, bethink thee of thy birth,
Call home thy ancient thoughts from banishment
And banish hence these abject lowly dreams.
Look how thy servants do attend on thee.
Wilt thou have music? *hark!* Apollo plays,   listen

[Music]

And twenty caged nightingales do sing:
Or wilt thou sleep? we'll have thee to a couch.
Say thou wilt walk; we will *bestrew the ground:*   strew flowers
Or wilt thou ride? Thy horses shall be trapp'd,
Their harness studded all with gold and pearl.
Dost thou love hawking? Thou hast hawks will soar
Above the morning lark or wilt thou hunt?
Thy hounds shall make the *welkin* answer them.   sky

FIRST SERVANT: Say thou wilt course; thy greyhounds are as swift
As *breathed stags*, ay, fleeter than the roe.   rested male deer

SECOND SERVANT: Dost thou love pictures? We will fetch thee straight
Adonis painted by a running brook,
And *Cytherea* all in sedges hid,   Venus, goddess of love
Which seem to move and wanton with her breath,

Even as the waving sedges play with wind.

LORD: Thou art a lord, and nothing but a lord:
Thou hast a lady far more beautiful
Than any woman in this waning age.

FIRST SERVANT: And till the tears that she hath shed for thee
Like envious floods o'er-run her lovely face,
She was the fairest creature in the world;
And yet she is inferior to none.

SLY: Am I a lord? and have I such a lady?
Or do I dream? or have I dream'd till now?
I do not sleep: I see, I hear, I speak;
I smell sweet *savours* and I feel soft things: odors
Upon my life, I am a lord indeed
And not a tinker nor Christopher Sly.
Well, bring our lady hither to our sight;
And once again, a pot o' the smallest ale.

SECOND SERVANT: Will't please your mightiness to wash your hands?
O, how we joy to see your wit restored!
O, that once more you knew but what you are!
These fifteen years you have been in a dream;
Or when you waked, so waked as if you slept.

SLY: These fifteen years! by my *fay*, a goodly nap.   faith
But did I never speak of all that time?

FIRST SERVANT: O, yes, my lord, but very *idle* words   silly
Sometimes you would call out for Cicely Hacket.

SLY: Ay, the woman's maid of the house.

THIRD SERVANT: Why, sir, you know no house nor no such maid,
Nor no such men as you have reckon'd up,
As Stephen Sly and did John Naps of Greece
And Peter Turph and Henry Pimpernell
And twenty more such names and men as these
Which never were nor no man ever saw.

SLY: Now Lord be thanked for my good *amends*!   recovery

ALL: Amen.

SLY: I thank thee: Thou shalt not lose by it.

[Enter the Page as a lady, with attendants]

PAGE: How fares my noble lord?

SLY: Marry, I fare well for here is cheer enough.
Where is my wife?

PAGE: Here, noble lord: What is thy will with her?

SLY: Are you my wife and will not call me husband?
My men should call me 'lord:' I am your *goodman*.   husband

PAGE: My husband and my lord, my lord and husband;
I am your wife in all obedience.

SLY: I know it well. What must I call her?

LORD: Madam.

SLY: Al'ce madam, or Joan madam?

LORD: 'Madam,' and nothing else: so lords call ladies.

SLY: Madam wife, they say that I have dream'd
And slept above some fifteen year or more.

PAGE: Ay, and the time seems thirty unto me,
Being all this time abandon'd from your bed.

SLY: 'Tis much. Servants, leave me and her alone.
Madam, undress you and come now to bed.

PAGE: Thrice noble lord, let me *entreat* of you   request
To pardon me yet for a night or two,
Or, if not so, until the sun be set:
For your physicians have expressly charged,
In peril to *incur* your former malady,   bring on
That I should yet absent me from your bed:
I hope this reason stands for my excuse.

SLY: Ay, it stands so that I may hardly *tarry* so long. But   wait
I would be loath to fall into my dreams again: I will
therefore tarry in despite of the flesh and the blood.

[Enter a Messenger]

MESSENGER: Your honour's players, heating your *amendment*,   recovery
Are come to play a pleasant comedy;
For so your doctors hold it very meet,
Seeing too much sadness hath congeal'd your blood,
And melancholy is the nurse of frenzy:
Therefore they thought it good you hear a play
And frame your mind to mirth and merriment,
Which bars a thousand harms and lengthens life.

SLY: Marry, I will, let them play it. Is not a
comonty a Christmas *gambold* or a tumbling-trick?   comedy/frolic

PAGE: No, my good lord; it is more pleasing stuff.

SLY: What, household stuff?

PAGE: It is a kind of history.

SLY: Well, well see't. Come, madam wife, sit by my side
and let the world slip: we shall ne'er be younger.

[Flourish]

Here the characters watch a play called The Taming of the Shrew, and we only hear from Sly and the lords
once more, very briefly.

Irresistible Shakespeare Scholastic Professional Books

A Midsummer Night's Dream
The Course of True Love Never Did Run Smooth

On the Reproducible

A scene adapted from acts 2 and 3 of *A Midsummer Night's Dream*

Background

A Midsummer Night's Dream is one of Shakespeare's most popular plays and certainly one that can be read very successfully with younger students. Both the romantic comedy and the magical fairy world can be wonderfully enticing for students.

The Midsummer's Eve referred to in the title marks the summer solstice. The Midsummer's Eve, according to Stephen Greenblatt in *The Norton Shakespeare,* was traditionally a time of "fairy tales and temporary madness." Shakespeare's tale is set in the classical world of Athens but, of course, features strong overtones of Elizabethan England. In the play, Shakespeare gives the nature of love and desire a close but comic look. There are four young lovers; two young men fall in love with one woman and then another. It takes much sorting out and help from the fairy world before "every Jack has his Jill," as Puck says at the end.

As you will notice if you are familiar with *Midsummer,* the mechanicals have been excised from this scene to achieve a reproducible length. The storyline of Titania falling in love with Bottom appears, regrettably, in a truncated form.

Focal Points for Exploration

⊚ The lyricism and high art of Shakespeare's language is especially evident here. The scene features rhymed iambic pentameter, which is somewhat unusual. Students will also be exposed here to rhymed trochaic tetrameter, which occurs, as is typical, with fairy speech. The fairy speech itself is often irregular and full of reversed feet.

⊚ The fairy world presented in the play creates abundant opportunities for imaginative flights of fancy. As you read the play, ask students to imagine the size and scale of the fairy world. Talented illustrators in your class might enjoy trying to draw what Shakespeare describes, such as the elves hiding in acorn shells to avoid the fighting between Titania and Oberon.

⊚ Students will certainly notice that within the comic tale of love gone awry some interesting questions are presented. How powerful are the forces of love and desire? How do they affect our ability to think rationally? How can we know when we are really in love? What is love?

Discussion Questions

1 In the beginning of the scene, which speech contains significant exposition (where a character provides the back story or fills the audience in on what is happening)? *Puck explains the argument between Titania and Oberon.*

2 How big are the elves? *Since Puck refers to them hiding in acorn shells we can assume they are quite tiny, perhaps under an inch high.*

3 Why does Oberon want Puck to get that certain flower he showed him once? *So that he can use it to punish Titania; he will put the juice in her eyes and make her fall in love with some unsuitable creature.*

4 How does Helena make a heaven of hell? *By being with her adored Demetrius, which is*

heaven, even though he spurns her cruelly, which is hell.

5 Why does Hermia want Lysander to sleep further off? *They are not yet married.*

6 Why does Hermia think Demetrius killed Lysander? *Demetrius was supposed to marry Hermia before she and Lysander escaped to the woods to avoid a forced marriage. Hermia thinks Demetrius has slain his rival.*

7 What line best sums up Puck's attitude toward the human world? *"Lord what fools these mortals be."*

8 Why does Helena think the others are plotting against her? *Just recently both Demetrius and Lysander were not interested in her and now they both are in love with her. She thinks that they, together with Hermia, are having fun at her expense. (She is unaware of the fairy world's intervention.)*

Related Activities

Acting It Out

This playlet provides a rich opportunity for interpretation. Students will need to create fairy characters and voices. They will get to play characters who run around madly with little clue about what is really happening. And finally there is a great catfight at the end of the playlet. Having the chance to act out this play is a great reward for the work of reading Shakespeare carefully.

Explaining the Unexplainable

In *A Midsummer Night's Dream* it appears that the secret doings of the fairy world may well be to blame for any number of human mysteries, from why milk curdles to why people suddenly fall out of love. Invite students to invent their own invisible, mysterious creatures who affect human lives. In a creative piece of at least one page, have students describe these creatures and their world and how their existence explains the unexplainable. The existence of these might offer the answers to questions such as: Why does it often rain at funerals? Why do machines break when we are rushing? Where are all the lost

objects of the world? And, in particular, where are all the missing single socks? These socks might, for example, be used by extraterrestrials as bandages, or perhaps very small, but long creatures steal them to use as sleeping bags. Encourage students to describe their creatures and their world in great detail.

Trading Insults

As the characters in the play fight, they trade wonderfully creative and original insults and expressions. Lysander, for example, is an inventive name-caller; he says to Hermia: "Get you gone, you dwarf/You minimus, of hindering knot-grass made,/You bead, you acorn." Have students write a short dramatic scene in which two characters argue and trade insults in a manner inspired by Shakespeare's characters. Students should try to create their own fantastically original insults. They will have to be inventive; there should be no common insults and no curses.

Art Projects

Midsummer lends itself beautifully to supplemental art projects. Students who do not want to act in scenes could work on a related art project.

- **Costume design:** Have students design a set of costumes for all the characters. Ask students to come up with a group of costumes for both the fairies and the humans. Remind them to think about whether or not the production they are designing for would be modern-dress production. Encourage them to imagine a color scheme for the whole production.

- **Stage design:** Have students come up with a set design that they make in a diorama. To make the diorama, they can use paints, clay, and any number of household items.

- **Dance:** The madness between the lovers could become a dance piece. Or students might want to choreograph a dance of the fairy world.

- **Comic book:** Have students reduce the story to key elements and illustrate it in comic-book form.

A Midsummer Night's Dream

The Course of True Love
Never Did Run Smooth

Who's Who?

PUCK, a mischievous fairy

FAIRY

OBERON, king of fairies

TITANIA, queen of fairies

HELENA, in love with Demetrius

DEMETRIUS, suitor to Hermia

LYSANDER, loved by Hermia

HERMIA, in love with Lysander

What's Happening?

The Fairy World: Oberon, the king of fairies, and Titania, the queen of fairies, are at odds with each other. Titania has a changeling, a child stolen by fairies. Oberon wants the boy, but Titania will not give him up. Oberon wants to punish her and sends Puck for a powerful flower that will cause her to fall in love with an unsuitable creature.

The Human World: A girl named Hermia has gone against her father's wishes in her choice of husband. She wants to marry Lysander, but her father wishes her to marry Demetrius, which she must do or die. The lovers Hermia and Lysander have fled to the forest. Unbeknownst to them, they have been followed there by Helena and Demetrius, who were formerly involved. Helena is still in love with Demetrius and follows him everywhere, driven crazy as she is by love.

As you will soon see, fairy and human worlds collide when Oberon is outraged to overhear Demetrius cruelly reject the beautiful Helena.

A wood near Athens.

Enter, from opposite sides, a Fairy, and PUCK

PUCK: How now, spirit?

FAIRY: Our queen and all her elves come here anon.

PUCK: The king doth keep his *revels* here to-night: entertainments
Take heed the queen come not within his sight;
For Oberon is passing *fell and wrath,*   dangerously angry
Because that she as her attendant hath
A lovely boy, stolen from an Indian king;
She never had so sweet a *changeling;*   child stolen by fairies
And jealous Oberon would have the child
Knight of his train, to trace the forests wild;
But she *perforce* withholds the loved boy,   by force
Crowns him with flowers and makes him all her joy:
And now they never meet in grove or green,
By fountain clear, or spangled starlight sheen,
But, they do *square, that* all their elves for fear   quarrel/ so that
Creep into acorn-cups and hide them there
But, room, fairy! Here comes Oberon.

FAIRY: And here my mistress. Would that he were gone!

[Enter, from one side, OBERON, with his
train; from the other, TITANIA, with hers]

OBERON: Ill met by moonlight, proud Titania.

TITANIA: What, jealous Oberon! Fairies, skip hence:
I have *forsworn* his bed and company.   sworn off

OBERON: Why should Titania cross her Oberon?
I do but beg a little changeling boy,
To be my *henchman.*   page or servant

TITANIA: Set your heart at rest:
The fairy land buys not the child of me.
His mother was a *vot'ress* of my order: sworn follower
And, in the spiced Indian air, by night,
Full often hath she gossip'd by my side.
But she, being mortal, of that boy did die;
And for her sake do I rear up her boy,
And for her sake I will not part with him.

OBERON: Give me that boy, and I will go with thee.

TITANIA: Not for thy fairy kingdom. Fairies, away!
We shall *chide downright,* if I longer stay.   argue outright

[Exit TITANIA with her train]

OBERON: Well, go thy way: Thou shalt not from this grove
Till I torment thee for this injury.
My gentle Puck, come hither.
Fetch me that flower; the herb I showed thee once:
The juice of it on sleeping eye-lids laid
Will make or man or woman madly dote
Upon the next live creature that it sees.

PUCK: I'll put a *girdle* round about the earth   circle
In forty minutes.

[Exit]

Irresistible Shakespeare Scholastic Professional Books

OBERON: Having once this juice,
I'll watch Titania when she is asleep,
And drop the liquor of it in her eyes.
The next thing then she waking looks upon,
Be it on lion, bear, or wolf, or bull,
On meddling monkey, or on busy ape,
She shall pursue it with the soul of love.
But who comes here? I am invisible;
And I will overhear their conference.

[Enter DEMETRIUS, HELENA, following him. Demetrius is Helena's former boyfriend. He has left her for a girl called Hermia, but Helena is still in love with Demetrius.]

DEMETRIUS: I love thee not, therefore pursue me not

HELENA: You draw me, you hard-hearted *adamant*.   hard, magnetic stone

DEMETRIUS: Do I entice you? Do I speak you fair?
Or, rather, do I not in plainest truth
Tell you, I do not, nor I cannot love you?

HELENA: And even for that do I love you the more.
I am your spaniel; and, Demetrius,
The more you beat me, I will *fawn* on you.   dote

DEMETRIUS: Tempt not too much the hatred of my spirit;
For I am sick when I do look on thee.

HELENA: And I am sick when I look not on you.

DEMETRIUS: I'll run from thee and hide me in the *brakes*,   thickets
And leave thee to the mercy of wild beasts.

HELENA: Your wrongs do *set a scandal on* my sex: scandalize
We cannot fight for love, as men may do;
We should be wooed and were not made to woo.

[Exit DEMETRIUS]

I'll follow thee and make a heaven of hell,
To die upon the hand I love so well.

[Exit HELENA]

OBERON: Fare thee well, nymph: *ere* he do leave this grove,   before
Thou shalt fly him and he shall seek thy love.

[Re-enter PUCK]

Hast thou the flower there? Welcome, wanderer.

PUCK: Ay, there it is.

OBERON: I pray thee, give it me.
I know a bank where the wild thyme blows,
There sleeps Titania sometime of the night,
And with the juice of this I'll streak her eyes,
And make her full of hateful fantasies.

Take thou some of it, and seek through this grove:
A sweet Athenian lady is in love
With a disdainful youth: *anoint* his eyes;   apply it to
But do it when the next thing he espies
May be the lady: thou shalt know the man
By the Athenian garments he hath on.
Effect it with some care, that he may prove
More fond on her than she upon her love:
And look thou meet me *ere* the first cock crow.   before

PUCK: Fear not, my lord, your servant shall do so.

[Exit]

[Another part of the wood. Enter TITANIA, with her train]

TITANIA: Come, a fairy song, sing me now asleep;
Then to your offices and let me rest.

*[The Fairies sing. Titania sleeps. Enter OBERON who squeezes the flower on
TITANIA's eyelids. OBERON exits. A man with the head of an ass walks by.
Titania wakes, sees, and falls in love. She follows the beast off stage.]*

*[Enter LYSANDER and HERMIA. They have fled to the forest because Hermia
has disobeyed her father in refusing to marry Demetrius. She loves Lysander
and he loves her.]*

LYSANDER: Fair love, you faint with wandering in the wood
We'll rest us, Hermia, if you think it good.

HERMIA: Be it so, Lysander: find you out a bed;
For I upon this bank will rest my head.

LYSANDER: One turf shall serve as pillow for us both;
One heart, one bed, two bosoms and one *troth*.   pledge

HERMIA: Nay, good Lysander; for my sake, my dear,
Lie further off yet, do not lie so near.

LYSANDER: Here is my bed: sleep give thee all his rest!

[They sleep. Enter PUCK]

PUCK: Through the forest have I gone.
But Athenian found I none,
On whose eyes I might *approve*   test out
This flower's force in stirring love.
Night and silence.—Who is here?
Weeds of Athens he doth wear: clothes
This is he, my master said,
Despised the Athenian maid;
And here the maiden, sleeping sound,
On the dank and dirty ground.
Pretty soul! she *durst* not lie   dare
Near this lack-love, this kill-courtesy.
Churl, upon thy eyes I throw   crass, rude man

All the power this charm doth owe.
When thou wakest, let love forbid
Sleep his seat on thy eyelid:
So awake when I am gone;
For I must now to Oberon.

[Exit. Enter DEMETRIUS and HELENA, running after him]

HELENA: Stay, though thou kill me, sweet Demetrius.

DEMETRIUS: I charge thee, hence, and do not haunt me thus.

[Exit]

HELENA: O, I am out of breath in this *fond* chase!   foolish
The more my prayer, the lesser is my grace.
Happy is Hermia, wheresoe'er she lies;
For she hath blessed and attractive eyes.
But who is here? Lysander! on the ground!
Dead? or asleep? I see no blood, no wound.
Lysander if you live, good sir, awake.

LYSANDER: *[Awaking]* And run through fire I will for thy sweet sake.
Transparent Helena! Nature shows art,
That through thy bosom makes me see thy heart.
Where is Demetrius? O, how fit a word
Is that vile name to perish on my sword!

HELENA: Do not say so, Lysander; say not so
What though he love your Hermia? Lord, what though?
Yet Hermia still loves you: then be content.

LYSANDER: Content with Hermia! No; I do repent
The tedious minutes I with her have spent.
Not Hermia but Helena I love:
Who will not change a raven for a dove?

HELENA: Wherefore was I to this keen mockery born?

[Exit]

LYSANDER: She sees not Hermia. Hermia, sleep thou there:
And never mayst thou come Lysander near!

[Exit]

HERMIA: *[Awaking]* Help me, Lysander, help me! Do thy best
To pluck this crawling serpent from my breast!
Ay me, for pity! What a dream was here!
Lysander! what, removed? Lysander! lord!
What, out of hearing? gone? no sound, no word?
Alack, where are you speak, an if you hear;
Speak, of all loves! I *swoon* almost with fear.   faint

[Exit]

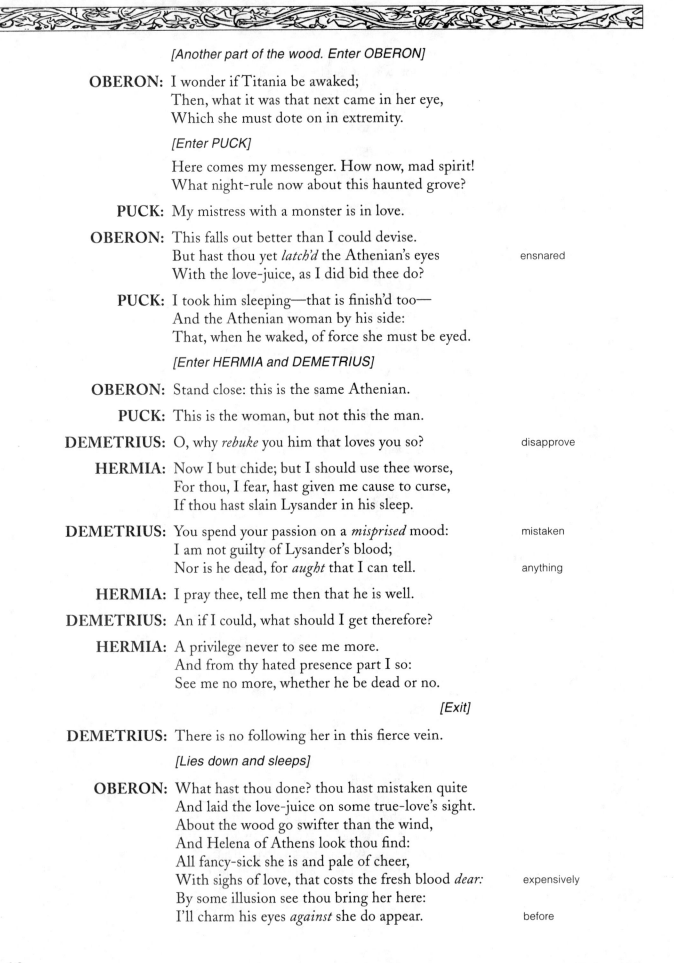

[Another part of the wood. Enter OBERON]

OBERON: I wonder if Titania be awaked;
Then, what it was that next came in her eye,
Which she must dote on in extremity.

[Enter PUCK]

Here comes my messenger. How now, mad spirit!
What night-rule now about this haunted grove?

PUCK: My mistress with a monster is in love.

OBERON: This falls out better than I could devise.
But hast thou yet *latch'd* the Athenian's eyes   ensnared
With the love-juice, as I did bid thee do?

PUCK: I took him sleeping—that is finish'd too—
And the Athenian woman by his side:
That, when he waked, of force she must be eyed.

[Enter HERMIA and DEMETRIUS]

OBERON: Stand close: this is the same Athenian.

PUCK: This is the woman, but not this the man.

DEMETRIUS: O, why *rebuke* you him that loves you so?   disapprove

HERMIA: Now I but chide; but I should use thee worse,
For thou, I fear, hast given me cause to curse,
If thou hast slain Lysander in his sleep.

DEMETRIUS: You spend your passion on a *misprised* mood: mistaken
I am not guilty of Lysander's blood;
Nor is he dead, for *aught* that I can tell.   anything

HERMIA: I pray thee, tell me then that he is well.

DEMETRIUS: An if I could, what should I get therefore?

HERMIA: A privilege never to see me more.
And from thy hated presence part I so:
See me no more, whether he be dead or no.

                             [Exit]

DEMETRIUS: There is no following her in this fierce vein.

[Lies down and sleeps]

OBERON: What hast thou done? thou hast mistaken quite
And laid the love-juice on some true-love's sight.
About the wood go swifter than the wind,
And Helena of Athens look thou find:
All fancy-sick she is and pale of cheer,
With sighs of love, that costs the fresh blood *dear:*   expensively
By some illusion see thou bring her here:
I'll charm his eyes *against* she do appear.   before

PUCK: I go, I go; look how I go,
Swifter than arrow from the Tartar's bow.

[Exit]

[Re-enter PUCK]

PUCK: Captain of our fairy band,
Helena is here at hand;
And the youth, mistook by me,
Pleading for a lover's fee.
Shall we their fond pageant see?
Lord, what fools these mortals be!

OBERON: Stand aside: the noise they make
Will cause Demetrius to awake.

[Enter LYSANDER and HELENA]

LYSANDER: Why should you think that I should *woo* in scorn?   court

HELENA: These vows *are Hermia's.*   belong to Hermia

LYSANDER: I had no judgment when to her I swore
Demetrius loves her, and he loves not you.

DEMETRIUS: *[Awaking]* O Helena, goddess, nymph, perfect, divine!
To what, my love, shall I compare thine eyne?

HELENA: O spite! O hell! I see you all are bent
To set against me for your merriment.
If you were men, as men you are in show,
You would not use a gentle lady so;
To vow, and swear, and superpraise my parts,
When I am sure you hate me with your hearts.

LYSANDER: You are unkind, Demetrius; be not so;
For you love Hermia; this you know I know:
And here, with all good will, with all my heart,
In Hermia's love I yield you up my part;
And yours of Helena to me *bequeath*,   pass on
Whom I do love and will do till my death.

HELENA: Never did mockers waste more idle breath.

DEMETRIUS: Lysander, keep thy Hermia; I will none:
If e'er I loved her, all that love is gone.
My heart to her but as guest-wise *sojourn'd*,   visited
And now to Helen is it home return'd,
There to remain.

LYSANDER: Helen, it is not so.

HERMIA: *[Entering]* What love could press Lysander from my side?

LYSANDER: Lysander's love, that would not let him bide,
Fair Helena, who more engilds the night
Than all you fiery *O's and eyes* of light.   stars

Why seek'st thou me? Could not this make thee know,
The hate I bear thee made me leave thee so?

HERMIA: You speak not as you think: it cannot be.

HELENA: Lo, she is one of this *confederacy!*   conspiracy
Now I perceive they have conjoin'd all three   joined with
To fashion this false sport, in spite of me.
Injurious Hermia! most ungrateful maid!
Have you conspired, have you with these contrived
To bait me with this foul *derision?*   ridicule
And will you rent our ancient love *asunder,*   in two
To join with men in scorning your poor friend?

HERMIA: I am amazed at your passionate words.
I scorn you not: it seems that you scorn me.

HELENA: Have you not set Lysander, as in scorn,
To follow me and praise my eyes and face?
And made your other love, Demetrius,
Who even but now did spurn me with his foot,
To call me goddess, nymph, divine and rare,
Precious, *celestial?*   heavenly

HERMIA: I understand not what you mean by this.

HELENA: Ay, do, *persever,* counterfeit sad looks,   continue
Make mouths upon me when I turn my back;   make faces at
Wink each at other; hold the sweet jest up.

LYSANDER: Stay, gentle Helena; hear my excuse:
My love, my life my soul, fair Helena!

DEMETRIUS: I say I love thee more than he can do.

LYSANDER: If thou say so, withdraw, and prove it too.

DEMETRIUS: Quick, come!

HERMIA: Lysander, whereto tends all this?

LYSANDER: Hang off, thou cat, thou burr! Vile thing, let loose,
Or I will shake thee from me like a serpent!

HERMIA: Why are you grown so rude? what change is this?
Sweet love,—

LYSANDER: Thy love! Out, tawny Tartar, out!
Out, loathed medicine! hated potion, hence!

HERMIA: Do you not jest?

LYSANDER: Be certain, nothing truer; 'tis no jest
That I do hate thee and love Helena.

HERMIA: [*To Helena*]O me! you *juggler!* you *canker-blossom!*   trickster/worm
You thief of love! What, have you come by night
And stolen my love's heart from him?

Irresistible Shakespeare Scholastic Professional Books

HELENA: Have you no modesty. What, will you tear
Impatient answers from my gentle tongue?
Fie, fie! you *counterfeit*, you puppet, you!   fake

HERMIA: Puppet? why so? ay, that way goes the game.
Now I perceive that she hath made compare
Between our statures; she hath urged her height;
And with her personage, her tall personage,
Her height, *forsooth*, she hath prevail'd with him.   in truth
And are you grown so high in his esteem;
Because I am so dwarfish and so low?
How low am I, thou painted maypole? speak;
How low am I? I am not yet so low
But that my nails can reach unto thine eyes.

HELENA: I pray you, though you mock me, gentlemen:
Let her not strike me. You perhaps may think,
Because she is something lower than myself,
That I can match her.

LYSANDER: Be not afraid; she shall not harm thee, Helena.

DEMETRIUS: No, sir, she shall not, though you take her part.

HELENA: O, when she's angry, she is keen and shrewd!
She was a vixen when she went to school;
And though she be but little, she is fierce.

HERMIA: 'Little' again! nothing but 'low' and 'little'!
Why will you suffer her to *flout* me thus?   mock
Let me come to her.

LYSANDER: Get you gone, you dwarf;
You *minimus*, of hindering *knot-grass* made;   tiny thing/weed
You bead, you acorn!

DEMETRIUS: You are too *officious*   presumptuous
In her behalf that scorns your services.

LYSANDER: Now follow, if thou darest, to try whose right,
Of thine or mine, is most in Helena.

DEMETRIUS: Follow! Nay, I'll go with thee, *cheek by jowl*.   side by side

[Exeunt LYSANDER and DEMETRIUS]

HELENA: I will not trust you, I,
Nor longer stay in your *curst* company.   cursed
Your hands than mine are quicker for a fray,
My legs are longer though, to run away.

[Exit]

HERMIA: I am amazed, and know not what to say.

[Exit]

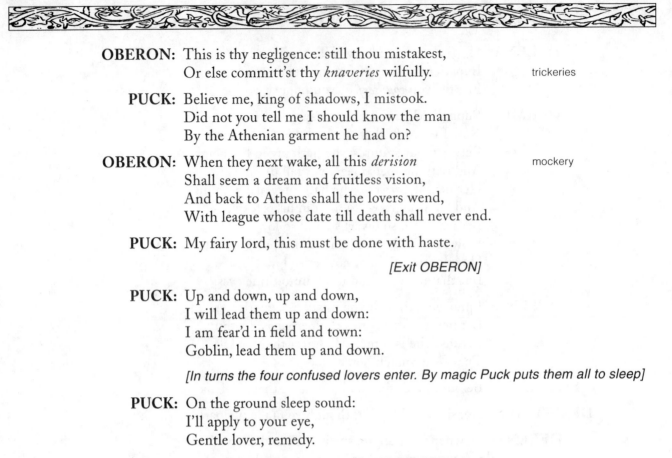

OBERON: This is thy negligence: still thou mistakest,
Or else committ'st thy *knaveries* wilfully.   trickeries

PUCK: Believe me, king of shadows, I mistook.
Did not you tell me I should know the man
By the Athenian garment he had on?

OBERON: When they next wake, all this *derision*   mockery
Shall seem a dream and fruitless vision,
And back to Athens shall the lovers wend,
With league whose date till death shall never end.

PUCK: My fairy lord, this must be done with haste.

[Exit OBERON]

PUCK: Up and down, up and down,
I will lead them up and down:
I am fear'd in field and town:
Goblin, lead them up and down.

[In turns the four confused lovers enter. By magic Puck puts them all to sleep]

PUCK: On the ground sleep sound:
I'll apply to your eye,
Gentle lover, remedy.

[Squeezing the juice on LYSANDER's eyes]

When thou wakest, thou takest
True delight in the sight
Of thy former lady's eye:
And the country *proverb* known,   old saying
That every man should take his own,
In your waking shall be shown:
Jack shall have Jill;
Nought shall go ill;   nothing
The man shall have his mare again, and all shall be well.

[Exit]

Romeo and Juliet
Two Blushing Pilgrims

On the Reproducible

A scene adapted from acts 1 and 2 of *Romeo and Juliet*

Background

Romeo and Juliet has been one of Shakespeare's most produced plays. Its theme of warring families brought together by the passion of youth has inspired productions set in a range of contexts, as well as various adaptations of the story line for the ballet and film, including *West Side Story*.

Shakespeare wrote *Romeo and Juliet* when he was relatively young. It certainly captures the impetuousness of young love.

In the scene excerpted here, we see a section of the play that is more comic in tone and full of hope. Romeo and Juliet meet for the first time and fall madly in love. Friar Laurence agrees to help the young lovers in the hopes that it will end the enmity between the two feuding families. Ultimately, the comic notes turn tragic as the rancor between the families intervenes and the play ends in the deaths of both Romeo and Juliet.

Focal Points for Exploration

◎ Pay special attention to the form in which Romeo and Juliet utter their first words to each other. The first 14 lines of their dialogue comprise a sonnet. You may want to introduce the sonnet to your students before reading this scene. Discuss with students Shakespeare's use of a sonnet in this scene. What quality does that rhyme scheme lend to their conversation from its opening words?

◎ Tragedy, in which things fall apart, is sometimes created through the raised hopes that things will work out—that all's well that ends well, as another play's title would have it.

The beginning of *Romeo and Juliet* has all the elements of romantic comedy. Then the story takes another turn and becomes a tragedy, though not within these pages. Ask students to speculate about why this section of the play has a strangely comic quality. Are there any hints to the tragedy that will occur?

Key Terms

comedy: a dramatic work with a light, usually humorous tone and subject matter, often involving the triumph of characters over adverse circumstances

tragedy: a serious dramatic work in which a protagonist is troubled by some terrible conflict that results in dire events

Discussion Questions

1 What is the mood at the masquerade ball as the scene opens? Ask students to imagine how the scene might look. *There is a general sense of excitement. The servants are bustling about and Capulet is in a merry mood.*

2 Why is Tybalt so angry about Romeo's appearance at the ball? *Romeo comes from the Montague family, the archrivals of the Capulets, Tybalt's family.*

3 At what point in the first 14 lines of conversation between Romeo and Juliet does Romeo kiss her? *After he says, "Then move not, while my prayer's effect I take."*

4 Why does Juliet wish Romeo had another name? *Because he would not be a Montague.*

5 Why does Friar Laurence agree to marry Romeo and Juliet? *So their love might unite their families.*

6 Why does Juliet become so impatient with her nurse when she returns from taking a message to Romeo? *Because the nurse seems to take forever in getting to the point.*

Related Activities

Playing with the Sonnet Form

Reread and discuss together the sonnet that appears when Romeo and Juliet meet for the first time. You might also share with students other examples of sonnets written by Shakespeare. Then, have students write a poem that uses the sonnet rhyme scheme *ababcdcdefefgg*. They should try to make all their lines about the same length and the final couplet should come to some conclusion or make some clear pronouncement about what has been discussed. If your students have become proficient in writing meter, you might add the additional component of writing in iambic pentameter.

Setting the Scene

In a tightly focused paragraph, ask students to respond to the questions: How does Shakespeare create the sense of the beginning of a real party in the opening scene? How does he create a festive mood? Ask them to be sure to write a strong generalization in the topic sentence and to use quotations at least twice in their paragraphs to support their points.

Love Story

There have been many versions of the Romeo and Juliet story. Invite students to write their own story about modern-day lovers who come from opposing worlds and fall madly in love. It can be a short story, or a mini-play and it might just introduce the characters, explain how they meet, and how they realize who the other person is.

Films Connections

Two interesting versions of *Romeo and Juliet* are available to supplement your study. One is the 1968 production by Franco Zeffirelli, which has a period setting; the other is a modern-dress production starring Leonardo DiCaprio and Claire Danes. Consider watching one of these or comparing how each version handled the scenes presented here.

Music Connections

Sergey Prokofiev composed a wonderful ballet for *Romeo and Juliet*. The theme to the Zeffirelli production of *Romeo and Juliet* became a radio favorite after it was released.

Romeo and Juliet
Two Blushing Pilgrims

Who's Who?

SERVANTS to the Capulet family

CAPULET, head of a large Venetian family, father of Juliet

SECOND CAPULET, a gentleman

ROMEO, son of Montague

TYBALT, nephew of Capulet's wife

JULIET, daughter of Capulet

NURSE, attendant upon Juliet

FRIAR LAURENCE, a member of the Franciscan Holy Order

What's Happening?

Before the scene begins, a young man named County Paris has asked permission to marry Juliet, who is not yet 14 and therefore too young for marriage. Her father, Capulet, however, promises her hand when she comes of age, *if* Paris truly finds her beauty extraordinary compared to other young women. Capulet therefore holds a masquerade ball that Juliet attends. The masquerade is the setting for the first scene. Romeo, who has been pining for a girl called Rosalind, shows up at the ball because he has learned she will be present. It is a fateful night for him; by the end of the evening Romeo has forgotten all about Rosalind.

Capulet's house. A masquerade ball is just beginning.

Musicians waiting. Enter servingmen with napkins

FIRST SERVANT:	Where's Potpan, that he helps not to take away? Away with the *joint-stools*, remove the *court-cupboard*, look to the plate. Good thou, save me a piece of *marchpane*.

        stools
        sideboard
        marzipan

SECOND SERVANT: Ay, boy, ready.

FIRST SERVANT: You are looked for and called for, asked for and sought for, in the great chamber.

SECOND SERVANT: We cannot be here and there too. Cheerly, boys; be
brisk awhile, and the longer liver take all.

*[Enter CAPULET, with JULIET and others of his house, meeting the Guests
and Maskers]*

CAPULET: Welcome, gentlemen! Ladies that have their toes
Unplagued with corns will have a *bout* with you.   dance
Ah ha, my mistresses! Which of you all
Will now deny to dance? She that *makes dainty*,   declines
She, I'll swear, hath corns; am I come near ye now?
Welcome, gentlemen! I have seen the day
That I have worn a visor and could tell
A whispering tale in a fair lady's ear,
Such as would please: 'tis gone, 'tis gone, 'tis gone:
You are welcome, gentlemen! Come, musicians, play.
A hall, a hall! give room! and foot it, girls.

Music plays, and they dance

More light, you *knaves*; and turn the tables up,   servants
And quench the fire, the room is grown too hot.
Ah, sirrah, this *unlook'd-for* sport comes well.   unexpected
Nay, sit, nay, sit, good cousin Capulet;
For you and I are past our dancing days:
How long is't now since last yourself and I
Were in a *masque*?   masquerade

SECOND CAPULET: By'r lady, thirty years.

CAPULET: What, man! 'tis not so much, 'tis not so much:
'Tis since the *nuptials* of Lucentio,   wedding
Come pentecost as quickly as it will,
Some five and twenty years; and then we mask'd.

ROMEO: *[To a Servingman]* What lady is that, which doth
enrich the hand
Of yonder knight?

SERVANT: I know not, sir.

ROMEO: O, she doth teach the torches to burn bright!
It seems she hangs upon the cheek of night
Like a rich jewel in an Ethiop's ear;
Beauty too rich for use, for earth too *dear*!   valuable
So *shows* a snowy dove trooping with crows,   appears
As yonder lady o'er her fellows shows.
The measure done, I'll watch her place of stand,
And, touching hers, make blessed my rude hand.
Did my heart love till now? forswear it, sight!
For I ne'er saw true beauty till this night.

TYBALT: This, by his voice, should be a Montague.
Fetch me my rapier, boy. What dares the slave
Come hither, cover'd with an *antic face*,   comic mask
To *fleer* and scorn at our solemnity?   sneer

Irresistible Shakespeare Scholastic Professional Books

Now, by the stock and honour of my kin,
To strike him dead, I hold it not a sin.

CAPULET: Why, how now, kinsman! Wherefore storm you so?

TYBALT: Uncle, this is a Montague, our foe,
A villain that is hither come in spite,
To scorn at our solemnity this night.

CAPULET: Young Romeo is it?

TYBALT: 'Tis he, that villain Romeo.

CAPULET: Content thee, gentle *coz*, let him alone;   kinsman
He bears him like a *portly* gentleman;   dignified
And, to say truth, Verona brags of him
To be a virtuous and well-govern'd youth:
I would not for the wealth of all the town
Here in my house do him *disparagement:*   disrespect
Therefore be patient, take no note of him:
It is my will, the which if thou respect,
Show a fair presence and put off these frowns,
And ill-beseeming *semblance* for a feast.   expression

TYBALT: It fits, when such a villain is a guest:
I'll not endure him.

CAPULET: He shall be endured.

TYBALT: Why, uncle, 'tis a shame.

CAPULET: *Go to*, go to.   go on
Be quiet, or—*[to the servants]* More light, more light!
[to Tybalt] For shame!
I'll make you quiet. *[to his guests]* What, cheerly, my hearts!

TYBALT: I will withdraw: but this intrusion shall
Now seeming sweet convert to bitter gall.

[Exit]

ROMEO: *[To JULIET, touching her hand]*
If I *profane* with my unworthiest hand   make unholy
This holy shrine, the gentle fine is this:
My lips, two blushing pilgrims, ready stand
To smooth that rough touch with a tender kiss.

JULIET: Good pilgrim, you do wrong your hand too much,
Which mannerly devotion shows in this;
For saints have hands that pilgrims' hands do touch,
And palm to palm is holy *palmers'* kiss.   pilgrims'

ROMEO: Have not saints lips, and holy palmers too?

JULIET: Ay, pilgrim, lips that they must use in prayer.

ROMEO: O, then, dear saint, let lips do what hands do;
They pray, grant thou, lest faith turn to despair.

JULIET: Saints do not move, though grant for prayers' sake.

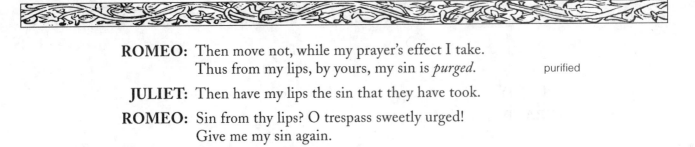

ROMEO: Then move not, while my prayer's effect I take.
Thus from my lips, by yours, my sin is *purged*.   purified

JULIET: Then have my lips the sin that they have took.

ROMEO: Sin from thy lips? O trespass sweetly urged!
Give me my sin again.

JULIET: You kiss by the book.

NURSE: Madam, your mother craves a word with you.

ROMEO: What is her mother?

NURSE: Marry, bachelor,
Her mother is the lady of the house,
And a good lady, and a wise and virtuous
I nursed her daughter, that you talk'd withal;
I tell you, he that can lay hold of her
Shall have the *chinks*.   money

ROMEO: Is she a Capulet?
O dear account! My life is my foe's debt.

[Exeunt all but JULIET and NURSE]

JULIET: Come hither, nurse. What is yond gentleman?

NURSE: The son and heir of old Tiberio.

JULIET: What's he that now is going out of door?

NURSE: Marry, that, I think, be young Petruchio.

JULIET: What's he that follows there, that would not dance?

NURSE: I know not.

JULIET: Go ask his name: if he be married.
My grave is like to be my wedding bed.

NURSE: His name is Romeo, and a Montague;
The only son of your great enemy.

JULIET: My only love sprung from my only hate!
Too early seen unknown, and known too late!
Prodigious birth of love it is to me,   ominous
That I must love a loathed enemy.

NURSE: What's this? what's this?

JULIET: A rhyme I learn'd even now
Of one I danced withal.

[One calls within 'Juliet.']

NURSE: Anon, anon!
Come, let's away; the strangers all are gone.

                              [Exit]

Irresistible Shakespeare Scholastic Professional Books

Capulet's orchard

[Enter ROMEO]

ROMEO: *[JULIET appears above at a window]*
But, soft! what light through yonder window breaks?
It is the east, and Juliet is the sun.
Arise, fair sun, and kill the envious moon,
Who is already sick and pale with grief,
That thou her maid art far more fair than she.
It is my lady, O, it is my love!
O, that she knew she were!
See, how she leans her cheek upon her hand!
O, that I were a glove upon that hand,
That I might touch that cheek!

JULIET: Ay me!

ROMEO: She speaks.
O, speak again, bright angel! for thou art
As glorious to this night, being o'er my head
As is a winged messenger of heaven
Unto the white-upturned wondering eyes
Of mortals that fall back to gaze on him
When he *bestrides* the lazy-pacing clouds   goes along
And sails upon the bosom of the air.

JULIET: O Romeo, Romeo! *Wherefore* art thou Romeo?   why
Deny thy father and refuse thy name;
Or, if thou wilt not, be but sworn my love,
And I'll no longer be a Capulet.

ROMEO: *[Aside]* Shall I hear more, or shall I speak at this?

JULIET: 'Tis but thy name that is my enemy;
Thou art thyself, though not a Montague.
What's Montague? it is nor hand, nor foot,
Nor arm, nor face, nor any other part
Belonging to a man. O, be some other name!
What's in a name? that which we call a rose
By any other name would smell as sweet;
So Romeo would, were he not Romeo call'd,
Retain that dear perfection which he *owes*   owns
Without that title. Romeo, *doff* thy name,   shed
And for that name which is no part of thee
Take all myself.

ROMEO: I take thee at thy word:
Call me but love, and I'll be new baptized;
Henceforth I never will be Romeo.

JULIET: What man art thou that thus bescreen'd in night
So stumblest on my *counsel?*   private thoughts

ROMEO: By a name
I know not how to tell thee who I am:
My name, dear saint, is hateful to myself,

Because it is an enemy to thee;
Had I it written, I would tear the word.

JULIET: My ears have not yet drunk a hundred words
Of that tongue's utterance, yet I know the sound:
Art thou not Romeo and a Montague?

ROMEO: Neither, fair saint, if either thee dislike.

JULIET: How camest thou hither, tell me, and wherefore?
The orchard walls are high and hard to climb,
And the place death, considering who thou art,
If any of my kinsmen find thee here.

ROMEO: With love's light wings did I o'er-perch these walls;
For stony limits cannot hold love out,
And what love can do that dares love attempt;
Therefore thy kinsmen are no *let* to me.   obstacle

JULIET: If they do see thee, they will murder thee.

ROMEO: Alack, there lies more *peril* in thine eye   danger
Than twenty of their swords: look thou but sweet,
And I am *proof* against their *enmity*.   armed/hatred

JULIET: I would not for the world they saw thee here.
By whose direction found'st thou out this place?

ROMEO: By love, who first did prompt me to inquire;
He lent me counsel and I lent him eyes.
I am no pilot; yet, wert thou as far
As that vast shore wash'd with the farthest sea,
I would *adventure* for such merchandise.   sail

JULIET: Thou know'st the mask of night is on my face,
Else would a maiden blush bepaint my cheek
Dost thou love me? O gentle Romeo,
If thou dost love, pronounce it faithfully:

ROMEO: Lady, by yonder blessed moon I swear
That tips with silver all these fruit-tree tops—

JULIET: O, swear not by the moon, the inconstant moon,
That monthly changes in her *circled orb*,   orbit
Lest that thy love prove likewise variable.

ROMEO: What shall I swear by?

JULIET: Do not swear at all;
Or, if thou wilt, swear by thy gracious self,
Which is the god of my idolatry,
And I'll believe thee.

ROMEO: If my heart's dear love—

JULIET: Well, do not swear: although I joy in thee,
I have no joy of this contract to-night:
It is too rash, too unadvised, too sudden;
Too like the lightning, which doth cease to be

Ere one can say 'It lightens.' Sweet, good night!   before
This bud of love, by summer's ripening breath,
May prove a beauteous flower when next we meet.
Good night, good night! as sweet repose and rest
Come to thy heart as that within my breast!

ROMEO: O, wilt thou leave me so unsatisfied?

JULIET: What satisfaction canst thou have to-night?

ROMEO: The exchange of thy love's faithful vow for mine.

JULIET: I gave thee mine before thou didst request it:
And yet I would it were to give again.

ROMEO: Wouldst thou withdraw it? for what purpose, love?

JULIET: But to be *frank*, and give it thee again.   honest
And yet I wish but for the thing I have:
My bounty is as boundless as the sea,
My love as deep; the more I give to thee,
The more I have, for both are infinite.

[Nurse calls within]

I hear some noise within; dear love, adieu!
Anon, good nurse! Sweet Montague, be true.
Stay but a little, I will come again.

[Exit, above]

ROMEO: O blessed, blessed night! I am afeard.
Being in night, all this is but a dream,
Too flattering-sweet to be substantial.

[Re-enter JULIET, above]

JULIET: Three words, dear Romeo, and good night indeed.
If that thy bent of love be honourable,
Thy purpose marriage, send me word to-morrow,
By one that I'll *procure* to come to thee,   obtain
Where and what time thou wilt perform the rite;
And all my fortunes at thy foot I'll lay
And follow thee my lord throughout the world.

NURSE: [*Within*] Madam!

JULIET: I come, anon.—But if thou mean'st not well,
I do beseech thee—

NURSE: [*Within*] Madam!

JULIET: By and by, I come:—
To cease thy suit, and leave me to my grief:
To-morrow will I send.

ROMEO: So thrive my soul—

JULIET: A thousand times good night!

[Exit, above]

ROMEO: A thousand times the worse, to want thy light.
Love goes toward love, as schoolboys from
    their books,
But love from love, toward school with heavy looks.

[Retiring]

[Re-enter JULIET, above]

JULIET: Hist! Romeo, hist! O, for a *falconer's* voice,   falcon trainer
To lure this tassel-gentle back again!
Bondage is hoarse, and may not speak aloud;
Else would I tear the cave where Echo lies,
And make her airy tongue more hoarse than mine,
With repetition of my Romeo's name.

ROMEO: It is my soul that calls upon my name:
How silver-sweet sound lovers' tongues by night,
Like softest music to attending ears!

JULIET: Romeo!

ROMEO: My dear?

JULIET: At what o'clock to-morrow
Shall I send to thee?

ROMEO: At the hour of nine.

JULIET: Good night, good night! parting is such
     sweet sorrow,
That I shall say good night till it be morrow.

[Exit above]

ROMEO: Sleep dwell upon thine eyes, peace in thy breast!
Would I were sleep and peace, so sweet to rest!
Hence will I to my ghostly father's cell,
His help to crave, and my dear hap to tell.

[Exit]

Friar Laurence's cell

[Enter FRIAR LAURENCE, with a basket]

[Enter ROMEO]

ROMEO: Good morrow, father.

FRIAR LAURENCE: *Benedicite!*   God bless you
What early tongue so sweet saluteth me?
Young son, it argues a *distemper'd* head   out of balance
So soon to bid good morrow to thy bed:
Care keeps his watch in every old man's eye,
And where care lodges, sleep will never lie;
But where unbruised youth with unstuff'd brain
Doth couch his limbs, there golden sleep doth reign:
Therefore thy earliness doth me assure
Thou art up-roused by some distemperature;

Or if not so, then here I hit it right,
Our Romeo hath not been in bed to-night.

ROMEO: That last is true; the sweeter rest was mine.

FRIAR LAURENCE: God pardon sin! Wast thou with Rosaline?

ROMEO: With Rosaline, my ghostly father? no;
I have forgot that name, and that name's woe.

FRIAR LAURENCE: That's my good son: But where hast thou been, then?

ROMEO: I'll tell thee, ere thou ask it me again.
I have been feasting with mine enemy

FRIAR LAURENCE: Be plain, good son, and homely in thy drift;
Riddling confession finds but riddling *shrift*.   absolution

ROMEO: Then plainly know my heart's dear love is set
On the fair daughter of rich Capulet:
As mine on hers, so hers is set on mine;
And all combined, save what thou must combine
By holy marriage: when and where and how
We met, we woo'd and made exchange of vow,
I'll tell thee as we pass; but this I pray,
That thou consent to marry us to-day.

FRIAR LAURENCE: Holy Saint Francis, what a change is here!
Is Rosaline, whom thou didst love so dear,
So soon forsaken? Young men's love then lies
Not truly in their hearts, but in their eyes.
Jesu Maria, what a deal of brine
Hath wash'd thy sallow cheeks for Rosaline!
How much salt water thrown away in waste,
To *season* love, that of it doth not taste!   preserve
The sun not yet thy sighs from heaven clears,
Thy old groans ring yet in my ancient ears;
Lo, here upon thy cheek the stain doth sit
Of an old tear that is not wash'd off yet:
If e'er thou wast thyself and these woes thine,
Thou and these woes were all for Rosaline:
And art thou changed? Pronounce this sentence then,
Women may fall, when there's no strength in men.

ROMEO: Thou chid'st me oft for loving Rosaline.

FRIAR LAURENCE: For doting, not for loving, pupil mine.

ROMEO: And bad'st me bury love.

FRIAR LAURENCE: Not in a grave,
To lay one in, another out to have.

ROMEO: I pray thee, *chide* not; she whom I love now   scold
Doth grace for grace and love for love allow;
The other did not so.

FRIAR LAURENCE: O, she knew well
Thy love did read by rote and could not spell.

But come, young waverer, come, go with me,
In one respect I'll thy assistant be;
For this alliance may so happy prove,
To turn your households' *rancour* to pure love.   ill will

ROMEO: O, let us hence; I *stand* on sudden haste.   depend

FRIAR LAURENCE: Wisely and slow; they stumble that run fast.

[Exit]

Capulet's orchard

[Enter JULIET]

JULIET: The clock struck nine when I did send the nurse;
In half an hour she promised to return.
Perchance she cannot meet him: that's not so.
O, she is lame! love's *heralds* should be thoughts,   messengers
Which ten times faster glide than the sun's beams.
Had she affections and warm youthful blood,
She would be as swift in motion as a ball;
My words would bandy her to my sweet love,
And his to me:
But old folks, many *feign* as they were dead;   act
Unwieldy, slow, heavy and pale as lead.
O God, she comes!

[Enter NURSE and PETER]
O honey nurse, what news?
Hast thou met with him? Send thy man away.

NURSE: Peter, stay at the gate.

[Exit PETER]

JULIET: Now, good sweet nurse,—O Lord, why look'st thou sad?
Though news be sad, yet tell them merrily;
If good, thou shamest the music of sweet news
By playing it to me with so sour a face.

NURSE: I am a-weary, give me leave awhile:
Fie, how my bones ache! what a *jaunt* have I!   running around

JULIET: I would thou hadst my bones, and I thy news:
Nay, come, I pray thee, speak; good, good nurse, speak.

NURSE: Jesu, what haste? can you not stay awhile?
Do you not see that I am out of breath?

JULIET: How art thou out of breath, when thou hast breath
To say to me that thou art out of breath?
The excuse that thou dost make in this delay
Is longer than the tale thou dost excuse.
Is thy news good, or bad? answer to that;
Say either, and I'll stay the circumstance:
Let me be satisfied, is't good or bad?

NURSE: Well, you have made a simple choice; you know not
how to choose a man: Romeo! No, not he; though his
face be better than any man's, yet his leg excels
all men's; and for a hand, and a foot, and a body,
though they be not to be talked on, yet they are
past compare: he is not the flower of courtesy,   beyond comparison
but, I'll warrant him, as gentle as a lamb. Go thy
ways, wench; serve God. What, have you dined at home?

JULIET: No, no: but all this did I know before.
What says he of our marriage? what of that?

NURSE: Lord, how my head aches! What a head have I!
It beats as it would fall in twenty pieces.
My back o' t' other side,—O, my back, my back!
Beshrew your heart for sending me about,   curse
To catch my death with jaunting up and down!

JULIET: I' faith, I am sorry that thou art not well.
Sweet, sweet, sweet nurse, tell me, what says my love?

NURSE: Your love says, like an honest gentleman, and a
courteous, and a kind, and a handsome, and, I
warrant, a virtuous,—Where is your mother?

JULIET: Where is my mother! why, she is within;
Where should she be? How oddly thou repliest!
'Your love says, like an honest gentleman,
Where is your mother?'

NURSE: O God's lady dear!
Are you so hot? Marry, come up, I trow;
Is this the poultice for my aching bones?
Henceforward do your messages yourself.

JULIET: Here's such a *coil!* come, what says Romeo?   commotion

NURSE: Have you got leave to go to *shrift* to-day?   confession

JULIET: I have.

NURSE: Then hie you hence to Friar Laurence' cell;
There stays a husband to make you a wife:
Now comes the wanton blood up in your cheeks,
They'll be in scarlet straight at any news.
Hie you to church; I must another way,
To fetch a ladder, by the which your love
Must climb a bird's nest soon when it is dark:
I am the drudge and toil in your delight,
But you shall bear the burden soon at night.
Go; I'll to dinner: hie you to the cell.

JULIET: Hie to high fortune! Honest nurse, farewell.

[Exeunt]

A Glossary for Shakespeare Studies

aside: when a character speaks his or her thoughts aloud but is not heard by the other characters on stage

blank verse: unrhymed iambic pentameter (Shakespeare often wrote in blank verse)

comedy: a dramatic work, usually light and humorous in tone and subject matter, often involving the triumph of characters over adverse circumstances

convention: a familiar practice made common by frequent usage

dramatis personae: literally the "persons of the drama," this is a list of the characters in the play

elision: a form in which two or three words are contracted when one word ends with a vowel and the next one begins with a vowel ("the express" becomes "th'express")

enjambment: when the syntax of a line carries into the next line of poetry

epilogue: in dramatic works, a speech, usually offered in verse, in which an actor addresses the audience at the end of the play

figurative language: language that makes use of figures of speech, especially metaphors

First Folio: the first anthology of Shakespeare's works, put together and published by his friends in 1623, seven years after the playwright died

the fourth wall: this refers to the boundary between the world of the play and the world of the audience. The phrase depicts the world of the play as a self-contained box or a room. When a character speaks directly to the audience, this is called "breaking the fourth wall." (For an example, see Rosalind's epilogue to *As You Like It.*)

heightened language: writing that is rich in imagery and poetic forms and is often metrical. Much of Shakespeare's work is considered to be heightened.

iamb: a disyllabic metrical unit in which the first syllable is unstressed and the second stressed

iambic pentameter: a metrical line of ten syllables comprising five metrical feet of iambs. Iambic pentameter is the most common meter in English poetry and drama and much of Shakespeare's plays are written in it.

in medias res: literally "in the middle of things"—when a scene or the play itself begins in the middle of things, before the plot has been laid out (for more on this, see "Cracking Open the Play")

meter: the regular rhythm that is created when syllables are stressed and unstressed in a systematic pattern

metaphor: a figure of speech, in which for the purposes of description, two unalike things are compared or equated

pastoral: scenes or settings that take place in the countryside, which often is idealized, and is in general peopled by shepherds and country folk

prologue: a speech at the beginning of the play that usually introduces the subject matter of the drama

protagonist: the character who is of leading importance in a drama or narrative

prose: language that is not written in meter and which is much more irregular in its rhythms than verse. Prose tends to be akin to what we would consider "normal" speech.

quarto: the single text publications of Shakespeare's plays that were printed during his lifetime, mostly illegally

scansion: the analysis of a line of verse in metrical terms

simile: a figure of speech in which unalike things are compared and connected by "like" or "as"

soliloquy: a dramatic monologue that often seems to express the internal, even secret workings of a character's mind

stock character: a familiar type of character who reflects very closely certain conventions, such as the "pantalone" of Italian comedy, the foolish old man who usually loves young girls

syncope: the contraction of a single word ("over" becomes "o'er)

tragedy: a serious dramatic work in which a protagonist is troubled by some terrible conflict that results in dire events

verse: used to describe lines written in metrical form, sometimes used simply to denote a piece of poetry

Works Consulted for this Glossary:

Sound and Sense by Laurence Perrine and Thomas R. Arp (HBJ, 1991)

Understanding Poetry by Cleanth Brooks and R. P. Warren (Holt, Hinehart & Winston, 1976)

Random House Unabridged Dictionary (Random House, 1987)

The Norton Anthology of English Literature (W.W. Norton, 1993)

Poetic Form, Poetic Meter by Paul Fussell (McGraw Hill, 1979)

The Wonders of Arden

As I walked into the Forest of Arden, I felt fairies dancing merrily on my heart. Then I felt the lightest and quietest wind encircle me and lift me high up into the skies. They reclined me on the softest, warmest, most beautiful white cloud you could ever imagine. It was so comfortable that I immediatly felt drowsy.

Then this quiet wind pushed me and the cloud to a magical waterfall. As the cool, crisp water trickled down my face and back, I saw all the animals holding a silk tapestry woven with flowers unknown to man. They encircled me and wrapped me with it, and the cloud brought me to the end, the end of the Forest of Arden.

Michael Magdovitz
Fifth grade
(written durring the 1998-1999 school year)